D1614260

COLORADO SPRINGS
FINE ARTS CENTER LIBRARY

*The
Ladies'
Work
Table*

Published on the occasion
of an exhibition of needlework
from the collection of
Professor and Mrs. Edwin Miller

September 25, 1988–January 8, 1989

The Ladies' Work Table

Domestic Needlework in Nineteenth-Century America

Margaret Vincent

ALLENTOWN ART MUSEUM
Allentown, Pennsylvania

Distributed by
University Press of New England
London and Hanover

1988

COLORADO SPRINGS
FINE ARTS CENTER LIBRARY

WITHDRAWN

COLORADO COLLEGE LIBRARY
COLORADO SPRINGS, COLORADO

On the cover: Suspenders. Probably Pennsylvania; 1890; canvas embroidered with multi-colored wool and metallic beads, trimmed with leather and elastic; 31″ by 2¼″

Designer: Tracy Baldwin
Editor: Jane Barry
Typesetter: Circle Graphics
Printer: Arcata Graphics/Kingsport Press
Photographer: Robert Walch

Copyright © Allentown Art Museum,
Allentown, Pennsylvania 18105

Library of Congress Cataloging-in-Publication Data

Vincent, Margaret.
    The ladies' work table.
    "Published on the occasion of an exhibition of needlework from the collection of Professor and Mrs. Edwin Miller, September 25, 1988–January 8, 1989."
    Bibliography: p. 137
    Includes index
    1. Needlework—United States—History—19th century. 2. United States—Social life and customs—19th century. I. Allentown Art Museum. II. Title.
TT705.V56 1988   746.4′0973   88-70509
ISBN 0-929011-39-2

20823
COLORADO SPRINGS
FINE ARTS CENTER LIBRARY

Mrs. Harry C. Trexler was one of the many women about whom this book speaks. Born Mary Mosser in 1852, she was the daughter of a Trexlertown, Pennsylvania, tanner, William K. Mosser and his wife, Lucy Fisher Mosser. In 1885 she married Harry Clay Trexler and became the perfect Victorian wife. She stood behind her husband in all his adventures, and although she was his advisor and confidant, she never asked to share his spotlight. Throughout her life she was an avid needlewoman. One of the founding members (in 1892) of the Allentown Branch of the Needlework Guild of America, she sewed and knitted garments for the hospitals and the needy of the Lehigh Valley. Despite crippling arthritis, Mrs. Trexler's favorite pastime was to make needlework gifts for family members and friends. She carried on her needlework traditions well into this century; a family friend remembered fondly how she used to sit listening to the radio while sewing. At her death in 1934, her estate joined her late husband's in what is now known as the Harry C. Trexler Trust. We are grateful to that organization for funding this catalogue and the exhibition that it accompanies in honor of Mrs. Harry C. Trexler.

Contents

Preface

America's decorative needlework of the eighteenth and early nineteenth centuries has a well-established antiquarian literature, and works of this period have lately enjoyed attention in highly specialized studies. Similarly, woven coverlets and pieced quilts made later in the nineteenth century have been the subject of numerous excellent studies and exhibitions. There has long been a need to extend this research, in a comprehensive way, to the end of the nineteenth century. The opportunity to supply a broad overview of American needlework through 1900 recently presented itself in the form of an exhibition based on the collection of Professor and Mrs. Edwin Miller.

Indefatigable in their search for superior examples of this material, the Millers are exceptional in that they also seek documentation of the context in which each object was produced. This is a highly laudable occupation for a collector; these mundane tasks are usually left to others to sort out, and frequently information is lost to history when an object leaves the family of its maker. *The Ladies' Work Table* is in part, the result of the Millers' scholarship and persistence.

The Allentown Art Museum's commitment to the study of textiles goes back to 1974, when we received by gift the large, impressive, and highly specialized collection of Kate Fowler Merle-Smith. Although ours is a small museum principally devoted to painting and sculpture, the Trustees were attentive to arguments that the economic history of the

Lehigh Valley was in no small way affected by and reflected in its textile industries. From the end of the eighteenth century through the demise of American silk weaving after World War II, the production of textiles was a primary local industry. Even today the Allentown district of the International Ladies Garment Workers Union boasts a membership of 5,100; coverlets locally woven at the beginning of the nineteenth century are among the most treasured heirlooms in many households between Easton and Kutztown.

The exhibition that introduced the Museum's new collection to the public was a world survey of the embroidered surface, capitalizing on the Merle-Smith collection's strengths in Eastern Mediterranean and Near Eastern folk embroideries. Curiously, Kate Fowler Merle-Smith herself showed little interest in American textiles, except for several splendid pieces made in Albany in the mid-eighteenth century that had descended in her family. The antiquarian craze for Americana spawned by the United States Centennial Exposition in Philadelphia in 1876 apparently affected her not in the least, though otherwise her interest in textiles was encyclopedic.

The family of Rosalind Schnitzer Miller, like many others, made its living and fortune in the local textile industry. Perhaps this was among the factors behind Mrs. Miller's enthusiasm as a collector. Professor and Mrs. Miller are long-time friends of the Allentown Art Museum. They have contributed substantially to the Museum's library and enriched the collections of prints and drawings, among other gifts. Yet their collection of American textiles was a revelation to me when I visited their home in New York about five years ago. Not only the theme of the collection, but its selectivity as well, came as a complete surprise. The abundance of documentary material was an additional pleasure.

The task of producing an exhibition and a catalogue surveying the American needlewoman's progress through the nineteenth century—comprehensively revealed in the Miller Collection, but heretofore explored only selectively—fell to the capable and disciplined care of Margaret Vincent, The Kate Fowler Merle-Smith Curator of Textiles. The results of Ms. Vincent's research in primary source material are represented in the lucid essay that follows. Her bibliography of nineteenth-century pattern books and needlework guides and guilds is unprecedented. It will undoubtedly inspire and inform researchers in the understudied field of post-1840 domestic arts; We hope therefore that *The Ladies' Work Table* may be regarded as a seminal effort rather than a definitive tome.

I express my unqualified thanks for the cooperative collaboration of Rosalind Miller and Margaret Vincent, who performed their respective roles as collector and scholar with great mutual esteem and, I would venture to guess, frequently great tact.

I am grateful to the Trustees of the Harry C. Trexler Trust for their enthusiastic support for this project. Once again the Trexler Trust has made possible the publication of original research initiated by the Allentown Art Museum, which will be useful well beyond the exhibition it serves immediately to document.

Peter F. Blume
Director

Collector's Notes

How and why collections are built is a question not easily answered. The momentum that propels the search—the motivation and excitement of acquisition—rests on many experiences over a lifetime. On reflection, there may even be a continuity of experiences that unwittingly shapes a collector's interests. At the age of five, I patiently awaited my mother's arrival home from her weekly needlework class, where she embroidered silk stitchery on silk in preparation for the making of lampshades. Needlework chairs and footstools worked by my mother filled our home. While "fancy" work was my mother's interest, "plain" work occupied my mother-in-law's leisure time: crocheted lace borders on pillow cases, crazy-patterned quilts, and crocheted tablecloths. Our daughter, an expert needlewoman, began to work crewel embroidery during her adolescence and later taught and designed needlework at the Women's Educational and Industrial Union in Boston. Together, we planned and creweled her wedding gown.

My husband and I have always been avid collectors, but it was not until some fifteen or more years ago that we began this collection of American embroidery and textiles. We were initially drawn to needlework purely as a decorative art—maybe as an extension of our mothers' world. As the collection grew, covering the period from the mid-eighteenth century through the first quarter of the twentieth, and as we pursued a more precise understanding of materials, technical aspects of execution, and iconographic sources, we were able to shape our questions and the collection itself in a more purposeful way.

An early area of inquiry was the relationship (if any) between the type of embroidery popular in an era and the changes occurring in the society over time. Were the particular types of needlework a phenomenon of the tides of taste, or did other factors shape the history of American needlework? Moreover, some arbiters of taste have stated that needlework, both in America and abroad, declined after 1830. We asked if this assertion was true, and, if so, how this decline occurred. In an attempt to answer these questions, we extended the collection into two additional areas.

One area involved our search for books, manuals, pamphlets, and magazines devoted to American needlework: samplers, embroidery, coverlets, quilts, lace, hooked rugs, clothing, linen, fabrics, and textiles. We were also interested in acquiring histories addressing eighteenth- and nineteenth-century American culture, social structure, family life, industrialization, subcultures, and sectionalism, especially as all of these affected women and the needlework they produced over a span of more than two hundred years.

At the same time, we initiated an on-going search for tools and materials in order to understand how each was used in the construction and execution of embroideries and needlework. This part of the collection includes such items as pins, needles, knitting needles, pin and needle keeps, sewing birds, swifts, niddy-noddies, marking stencils, hand-painted as well as printed patterns and designs, silk threads, and textiles, including examples of homespun, tow, cotton, and early American printed fabrics.

The core collection of needlework encompasses what was sewn by American women from varied social classes and cultures, and from urban and rural areas. Although the quality of the needlework has remained our primary criterion for selection, weight has also been given to an item's reflection of its historical period. Therefore we have not sought out only the rarest and most unique works. Our choices have also been influenced by the possibility of tracing a piece's provenance, maker, and date. This latter endeavor has allowed us to pursue the genealogical holdings of many historical societies. Acquisitions for the collection derive from driving the back roads of the eastern states from Pennsylvania to Maine; country auctions, long associations with individual dealers, and private individuals have provided us not only with needlework but with warm friendships.

This exhibition covers the years from 1800 to 1900 and pays tribute to the nineteenth-century woman. The hundred-year span saw sweeping social and industrial changes, the emergence of a mass society, revolutionary improvements in transportation, increased opportunities for women in education and employment, mass production and consumption of publications, and the growth of cultural pluralism with the arrival of multi-ethnic groups from Europe. All these influences had a marked impact on the needle arts. A reappraisal of the needlework of this period is needed, just as scholars and critics are currently revising our appreciation and understanding of nineteenth-century American art and furniture.

The linens, coverlets, quilts, rugs, clothing, and accessories selected for this exhibition provided the nineteenth-century woman with a means for self-expression and artistic pursuit. However elaborate or however plain, her handiwork is part of our American heritage.

My husband and I are privileged and gratified by Peter Blume's invitation to exhibit a part of our collection at the Allentown Art Museum. This is the first time we have released any part of the collection for public viewing, and it is all the more fitting and significant that this event takes place in Allentown, my birthplace. Discussion of the exhibition began several years ago, and the planning and selection process started in December 1986.

Major credit for this project must go to the vision and dedication of Margaret Vincent, the Museum's Kate Fowler Merle-Smith Textile Curator. Over a period of many months, she traveled at least weekly between Allentown and New York to work on the collection, studying each piece before the final selection was made. This was a prodigious undertaking, which she accomplished in an orderly, highly disciplined way, enriching us with her expertise and knowledge. The text of this catalogue attests to the breadth of her understanding. She was ably assisted by Linda Rehrig and by Robert Walch, who worked on the collection in our home. Robert Walch was responsible for the photography.

Many people have been involved in either finding or alerting us to the availability of items for purchase. We thank them all, and add a special note of gratitude to Elizabeth and Kenneth Berrett, Janette Kohli, and Frances Brown.

And, finally, our appreciation to the Harry C. Trexler Trust for its sponsorship of this exhibition.

Rosalind Schnitzer Miller

Introduction

This book began with a collection. In December of 1986 I was invited to visit the home of Professor and Mrs. Edwin Miller to see their needlework collection. After poring over some 1,000 pieces of embroidery and related artifacts, I agreed with Mrs. Miller that the collection would make an excellent exhibition. In our early conversations we discussed the purpose of such a display. Mrs. Miller was adamant that the exhibition and the accompanying catalogue should not only showcase artwork, but contain sufficient sociological and historical content as well. We also agreed that the existing collection should set the parameters of our study. The purpose, scope, and viewpoint are all expressed in our title, *The Ladies' Work Table: Domestic Needlework in Nineteenth-Century America.*

The scope of the Miller collection suggested that our study be limited to needlework. The term "needlework" is here used in the nineteenth-century sense. In 1882 Caulfeild and Saward defined it as "a generic and comprehensive term, including every species of work that can be executed by means of the Needle, whether plain or decorative, and of whatever description the Needle may be."[1] The emphasis of our study is on hand sewing, although many objects made in the latter half of the century do contain at least some machine work. Related crafts such as knitting, crochet, and lacemaking are included because they were generally considered needlework. Needlework materials such as

[1] Sophia Frances Anne Caulfeild and Blanche C. Saward, *The Dictionary of Needlework: An Encyclopedia of Artistic, Plain and Fancy Needlework* (London: A. C. Cowan, 1882), 354.

thread and fabric, even if made by the needleworker, are not treated in this volume. Although equally important and relevant within the same social and historical contexts, we feel that materials deserve a separate study.

The second parameter we set was geographical. With a few exceptions, the Millers collect works made in America. To the best of our knowledge, all the artifacts illustrated in this book are American. In researching and writing the text, however, we found it impossible to ignore what was happening in Europe. Throughout the nineteenth century, women's crafts were influenced by ideas, technology, materials, and designs that first emerged on the European continent or in Great Britain. By introducing these foreign subjects, we hope to provide a better understanding of the American works.

Because we use "America" in our title, some readers might assume that we intend to cover needlework made throughout the country. This is not the case. Except for an occasional piece from Kentucky or Virginia, the Miller collection is limited to works that were made in the rural and industrial Northeast. Similarly, most of the research material available to us comes from the Northeast. Nevertheless, this study does represent American needlework. All of America looked directly or indirectly to Philadelphia, New York, and Boston for fashion ideas. In photographs of pioneer women in remote western villages, we see crochet trims like those illustrated in the Philadelphia magazine *Godey's Lady's Book.* Fashionable silk crazy quilts were made in the Midwest and South as well as the Northeast. Even Native American crafts gave way (either by choice or by force) to the crafts of the eastern cities. We define as "American," therefore, the styles that were most widely known and widely copied.

There were, of course, many regional traditions in nineteenth-century America, far too many to cover adequately in a volume of this size. We have chosen to highlight three: hand towels, quilts, and hooked rugs. The hand towels, cross stitched by Pennsylvania German women, represent the many rich ethnic traditions prevalent throughout the nation. Pieced and appliquéd quilts, known in virtually every region of the country, reflect the growing differences between city and country life. Hooked rugs, which probably originated in Maine and surrounding areas, stand for local customs.

Setting the chronological boundaries of the study within the nineteenth century has caused both frustration and satisfaction. The Miller collection is not limited to nineteenth-century works, and some very fine examples had to be excluded simply because they were very clearly dated 1796 or 1909. Nor does the history of needlework begin exactly in 1800 and end abruptly in 1900. Yet the Miller collection is representative of the entire nineteenth century and therefore has allowed us to follow the evolution of embroidery through the full hundred years. Within this time period, styles and techniques continually evolved, and the needlework of each succeeding generation differed significantly from that of the last.

To show this evolution, we have divided the chronological presentation into four chapters. The first chapter deals with the Federal Era (1800–1830), a time of samplers and white work, plain sewing and ornamental work. In these decades *all* women sewed, but only wealthy women made elaborate decorative embroideries. The second chapter, on the period from 1830 to 1860, follows the emergence of the styles that we know as "Victorian," and particularly the canvas work now called "Berlin work." This was an era when the country saw major developments in industry, and the embroideries are those of the emerging entrepreneurial middle class. A transitional period, from 1860 to 1876, is covered in chapter 3, which describes how needlework was affected by the Civil War and the massive postwar technological revolution. Chapter 4 details the final quarter of the century (1876–1900), when American manufacturers and an expanded embroidering population reacted to the English Aesthetic Movement to produce a remarkably eclectic assortment of needlework patterns and techniques.

The variety of needlework styles practiced during the nineteenth century is astounding. This book is intentionally an overview and covers only the most popular forms. The text is not intended to be an in-depth study of any one method, but is meant to show how the various needlework forms related to each other chronologically and technically. Nor is this volume an instructional manual. For readers interested in replicating the nineteenth-century crafts, we offer as an appendix a list of manuals, many of which are available in modern reprint.

The present volume concentrates entirely on domestic needlework—that is, needlework made by women in the home. Works by children are included, even if made at school, since these embroideries were intended to train girls for domestic life. Our intention is to show works that were made either for the immediate family or as gifts for friends, relatives, or charities. The words "domestic" and "home" were important in the nineteenth-century vocabulary: "The sum of human happiness lies in the words 'Home making, Home keeping.' A home well made, well kept, well guarded is as near paradise as any earthly thing may be, and should be the subject of greatest importance in a woman's life from the hour she pronounces the fateful 'I will' to the one in which she yields up her charge and joins the 'throng innumerable.' "[2] Needlework played a large part in a woman's ability to be the ideal wife and mother, for through her needlework she provided clothing and necessary household furnishings. Through her choice of

[2] Adelaide E. Heron, *Dainty Work for Pleasure and Profit* (Chicago: Danks & Co., 1891), xvi.

patterns and mottoes, moreover, she could instill a strong sense of morals in her husband and children.

Where possible we have avoided using objects made by professionals, such as Baltimore Album quilts and fine laces. Rather, the works illustrated here are all very typical examples of a domestic art form and represent the wide range of artistic and technical abilities possessed by the women of nineteenth-century America. To show a selection of masterworks—that is, the best works made—would be to misrepresent an era. For every fine silk-embroidered picture, there were dozens of less impressive pictorial samplers. For every elaborate "best" quilt a woman made, she probably worked several everyday quilts. For each custom-made curtain designed by Candace Wheeler, the late nineteenth-century textile artist, there were hundreds of embroidered tea cloths. We seek to show not only the elite minority, but also the popular majority.

Some readers will be disappointed that the works illustrated here do not always show original designs. By including needlework that follows professional patterns, we seek to fight an elite, modern bias that always looks for what is new and unique. The nineteenth-century woman wanted to make objects that were fashionable and up to date, but she never considered it a handicap to be artistically untrained. In the early part of the century, women—with pride, not shame—paid artists to draw designs on cloth. In the middle of the century, few women made their own canvas work patterns, and fewer still embroidered without any pattern. In the later part of the century, women purchased commercial patterns or even partially worked embroideries with equal readiness.

One must remember that each work, even a seemingly mundane and unoriginal needlework piece, was considered a masterpiece by the woman who made it. The artist-craftswoman never expected that an audience a century or two later would be judging her work, but she was doing her best work, taking pride in her abilities. The truly original contributions of the artist are often subtle, but no less important. Tasteful choice of colors, ability to render shading and variations on a standard theme, are seen throughout the works. Readers are encouraged to look for these small signs of originality and to see the individuality of each artist.

The purpose of the exhibition and my personal viewpoint are suggested in our choice of "The Ladies' Work Table" as our primary title. This practical phrase was used as a title for a number of nineteenth-century books and magazine articles, the most important period source on which this study is based. Its use here reflects our goal of being true to the era. Histories of needlework have often been based on other histories and have included inaccuracies and obvious legends. The tradition of exaggerating or inventing can be traced back to the earliest histories, which weave long and complex stories around quotations from classical literature. While the myths may be fascinating, tales of Penelope and Minerva have little to do with the needlework of nineteenth-century America.

Finally, it was both Mrs. Miller's and my belief that needlework cannot be separated from the history of the country. The present volume is not just the story of patterns and stitches. It aims to set embroidery and other needle arts within a larger historical context. Political, social, aesthetic, and technological changes all affected the arts and crafts of the home. However, this work does not attempt to make the subject matter more important than it is. National and international events influenced needlework, but needlework did not change the world. The Civil War may have altered the forms of needlework, but needleworkers did not significantly alter the course of the war. The needle was very much a part of the family structure, but the needle did not define the cult of motherhood. The needlework illustrated here is, rather, a material record of individual women's responses to all these forces and events, to their families' needs, and to their own desire for self-expression.

My deepest thanks go to Professor and Mrs. Miller for allowing me to study and use their fine collection. Needlework is a family affair for the Millers. Mrs. Miller's daughter Pamela Ness has graciously lent six items from her own collection. It has been a pleasure to work with the Millers. Their efforts to secure suitable objects and to provide adequate documentation were particularly helpful. I also thank them for their kind hospitality during my many trips to their house.

I thank my director, Peter F. Blume, for the latitude that he has given me on this project. Through his support, we have been able to take a far more historically and sociologically oriented approach than one might expect in an art museum exhibition and catalogue. Many thanks are due to Linda Rehrig, my assistant, who spent unlimited hours cataloging and preparing the works for publication and exhibition. Without her this project would have been impossible. I give a collective thanks to all the staff of the Allentown Art Museum, each of whom played an important part in the completion of the catalogue and exhibition. Thanks also to the Society of the Arts, the Museum's volunteer corps, to Evie Pappas, and to our Lehigh University intern, Aileen Silverman.

Many libraries and archives provided assistance during the research phase of the project. I especially thank the staffs of the New York Public Library, the Free Library of Philadelphia, the Library of Congress, the Watson Library of the Metropolitan Museum of Art, the Doris Stein Research Center of the Los Angeles County Museum of Art, the Henry C. Trexler Library at Muhlenberg College, the Lehigh County Historical Society, and the Moravian Museum.

Large parts of this book rely heavily on the research of other scholars. The history of samplers is excellently covered by Davida Deutsch, Glee F. Krueger, Betty Ring, and Susan B. Swan. Of the many quilt scholars, I note particularly the work of Jeannette Lasansky, Penny McMorris, Patsy and Myron Orlofsky, and Jonathan Holstein. A definitive study of Pennsylvania German hand towels exists through the efforts of Ellen Gehret and others. The existence of these sources and others listed in the Selected Bibliography has allowed me to concentrate on areas that have been less well researched.

I am grateful to the Harry C. Trexler Trust for the generous grant that has funded this project. Continued financial support for the Textile Department has come from the family of Kate Fowler Merle-Smith, to which I owe enormous thanks. I acknowledge the National Endowment for the Arts, the Samuel H. Kress Foundation, The Century Fund, Mrs. William C. Hacker, and other donors for their contributions to the new facilities in which the exhibition was prepared. I thank the Institute of Museum Services for general operating support during the current year. As always, we are grateful to the Museum's corporate and general members, whose contributions make exhibitions possible. Finally, I am thankful for an anonymous donation that resulted in the acquisition of AT&T computer equipment, significantly easing manuscript preparation.

I am indebted to Tracy Baldwin for her excellent book design. She was able to instill just the right amount of levity into the subject matter and has given very professional service. I thank Suzanne Nelson for an insightful early reading of the manuscript and Jane Barry for her very fine editing. Many thanks to Robert Walch for his photography, Circle Graphics for typesetting, and Arcata Graphics/Kingsport Press for printing this book. Finally, I thank the University Press of New England for agreeing to distribute it to a much wider audience than we have previously been able to reach.

Margaret Vincent
The Kate Fowler Merle-Smith
Textile Curator

CHAPTER ONE

The Federal Era

1800–1830

*I*n 1800 the United States looked forward to a century of growth and change. The population was increasing at a rate of over 30 percent every ten years, as births were reinforced by immigration. The country would soon expand to include new territories. First canals and then the railroad would carry travelers westward. Educational systems were improving, giving each new generation a wider knowledge than the last. Available capital, abundant raw materials, new technology, and cheap labor would soon spawn an industrial age that few eighteenth-century people could have predicted.

Yet in 1800 the country still looked backward for its traditions and way of life. At least 95 percent of the population lived in rural areas. They raised crops, tended animals, and kept house in age-old ways. Despite the Revolution, cultural ties to Europe were strong. America was still not self-sufficient; it continued to import both materials and ideas from Europe. Medicine was primitive, as were systems of hygiene, and the death rate for infants was high. Still only a few decades old, the country searched for a national identity.

The nation had been founded as a democracy; theoretically Americans rejected a system of rank established through birth. Yet the country also encouraged accumulation of wealth, and this had led to a strong class system. Of the 5 million people inhabiting the eastern seaboard, less than 5 percent were affluent enough to be considered wealthy. The class system presents a problem in the history of needle-work. Nearly all women sewed. Yet most of the extant embroideries belonged to wealthy citizens. In addition, most of the written documentation refers to the same group. A discussion of the needlework of this period, therefore, contains two parts: that of the wealthy, about whom we know a great deal, and that of the less wealthy, about whom we know little.

Among the upper classes were the families of successful northern merchants and southern plantation owners. While the men worked in their respective businesses, the women lived a life of leisure, spending their days overseeing servants or slaves. Although few were first-generation Americans, these wealthy women still looked to Europe for their domestic goods, for their aesthetic taste, and for their lifestyle. They imported fine silks from China and muslins from India. They copied English lithographs, French fashion plates, and European interior design. Needlework was an accomplishment required of every well-bred young lady.

The vast majority of Americans fell into the middle- or lower-income classes. They lived in rural areas, small towns, or crowded neighborhoods in the eastern cities. For these people life moved slowly, perhaps, but conditions were far from idyllic. The average daily routine for the women consisted of household chores: cooking, cleaning, spinning, weaving, and sewing. Women sewed not by choice, but because they had to. They needed to clothe themselves and their families and furnish their houses. Imported materials and ready-made goods were usually beyond their means. Their design inspiration was the same as that of the wealthy, yet because they received it at second hand, both a time lag and a simplification of fashionable ideas are apparent.[1]

Learning to Sew

At the beginning of the nineteenth century, all girls, regardless of economic or social circumstance, learned to sew. If her father could afford it, a girl was enrolled in a formal or informal private school. These institutions varied greatly in size, in curriculum, and in the competence of the teachers. To complement standard academic subjects such as geography and history, most schools offered the more refined arts of dancing, music, drawing, and needlework. Needlework training included instruction in practical and ornamental work.[2]

The schools attended by wealthy girls in the first years of the nineteenth century did not differ significantly from those that their mothers and grandmothers attended in the latter part of the eighteenth century. However, the number as well as the geographical availability of schools increased after 1800, and a progressively larger number of families

[1] Among the less affluent were groups who retained their own non-Anglo ethnographic traditions. Their design inspiration, of course, relied less on aristocratic taste than on their own folk culture. See, for example, the discussion of Pennsylvania German hand towels in chapter 5.

[2] For further information about schools, see Glee F. Krueger, *New England Samplers to 1840* (Sturbridge, Mass.: Old Sturbridge Village, 1978); and Betty Ring, *Let Virtue Be a Guide to Thee: Needlework in the Education of Rhode Island Women, 1730–1830* (Providence: Rhode Island Historical Society, 1983).

began to educate their daughters. The nineteenth century also saw the beginning of public and charity schools, which were open to large numbers of girls despite or even because of their parents' modest financial status.

It is impossible to know exactly how many girls received their needlework training in a formal classroom setting. Perhaps 10 to 30 percent of all girls whose childhoods fell between 1800 and 1830 benefited from such education. The remaining girls were taught by their mothers, grandmothers, older siblings, employers, or (in the case of slaves) owners. Training within the home emphasized practical sewing, which would be required in adult life. Many girls learned to sew seams by stitching small fabric scraps together to form doll-size quilts. Some may have learned embroidery and made simple samplers, if they or their instructors were familiar with the art form.

Plain Work

The first stitches a girl learned were utilitarian. There were three forms of "plain," "common," or "useful work": sewing, mending, and knitting. Sewing comprised simple tasks like hemming and seaming as well as more difficult jobs such as making buttonholes (fig. 1). Since materials were scarce, women continually mended, darned, or patched holes, trying to make garments and furnishings last as long as possible. Knitting, although it employed different skills, was considered plain work: the knitter manufactured a functional, rather than a decorative, object (fig. 2). The words "practical" and "necessary" were often used in instruction manuals in conjunction with plain sewing, mending, and knitting.

During the first three decades of the nineteenth century, all plain sewing was accomplished by hand.[3] It is wrong, however, to assume that all items made by hand were made at home. Generally, if the household could afford it, better clothing and furnishings were sewn by a hired professional. The work of professionals is difficult to identify in this era because few tailors or seamstresses signed their work and because training in cutting and sewing techniques was similar for professionals and nonprofessionals.

Still, there were a number of furnishings and garments that women traditionally made at home. Most household linens were of home manufacture. Among these were sheets, pillowslips, bed coverings, towels, and table mats. Home-made clothing consisted mostly of personal linens. For her own use, a woman sewed underclothing, caps, bags, pockets, aprons, and the like (figs. 3, 4). For her husband, she produced shirts, handkerchiefs, and (occasionally) underdrawers. If a mother, she invariably sewed all the garments worn by her infant and

[3] Although some inventors had attempted a machine that could sew seams, no viable tool was produced in sufficient quantity during the first half of the century to have an impact on plain sewing.

1

Although early nineteenth-century American women preferred to have their clothing professionally made, they usually sewed their own personal linens. The long vertical seams, the hem, and the gathering at the waist of this cotton petticoat constituted plain sewing. The skilled maker of this garment added a subtle but effective trim. Note the rick rack (detail) which was made by folding and sewing together a narrow woven tape.

USA; ca. 1830; white cotton; 36″ long

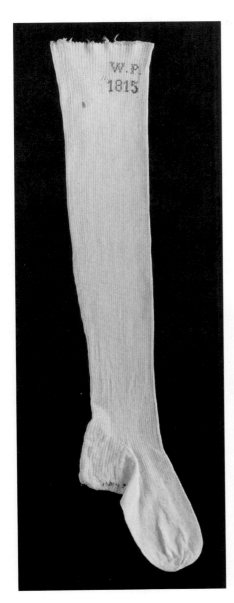

2

Knitting, although it might include some fancy stitches, was primarily a very practical craft. This well-worn pair of cotton stockings, found in a home in Moravia, New York, bears the initials "W. P." and the date 1815, which have been cross stitched in red cotton thread (probably later in the century). The stockings also illustrate the importance of darning and patching, which were taught along with plain sewing. Moravia, N.Y.; 1815; white cotton, embroidered with red cotton; 31″ long

3

Throughout the first half of the nineteenth century, most American women wore muslin caps every day. The home-made caps changed very little from decade to decade, since old caps were cut apart to provide patterns for new ones. Because the cap was quite visible, the stitching was often fine, even if the cut was simple. This example shows the talents of Lorinda Paton, whose name is penned in brown ink on the corner. New England; early 19th c.; white linen or cotton; 19½″ by 8″

pre-teenaged children. No commercial patterns and no books or magazine articles were available to the home sewer. Patterns were most likely drawn freehand, or copied from an existing object. If she considered herself completely inept or if she wanted a professional look for her work, a woman took her cloth to a seamstress or tailor to be cut.

Embroidered Letters

After mastering stitches that were structural in nature, a girl moved on to "fancy," "fine," or "ornamental work" and completed one or more samplers (fig. 5). In its simplest form, a sampler contained only alpha-

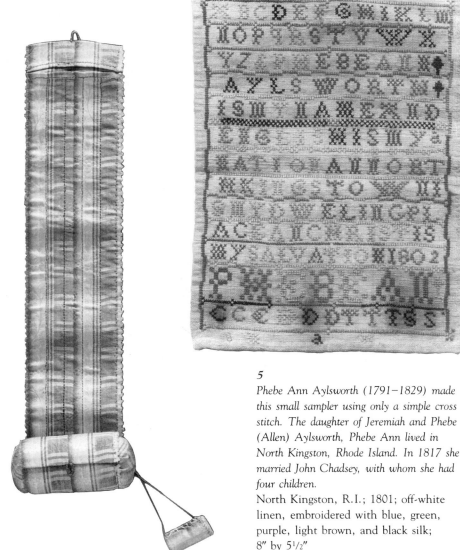

4
The high cost of needles and pins probably led to the invention of this item, a needle keep. Made from silk brocade ribbons, the case contains a legend written by Eliza Green: "This little token of affection was given me by my early friend Mary Appleton (now Mrs. John Aiken) in 1823 for a wedding present—I value it above rubies." Mary Appleton was the sister-in-law of President Franklin Pierce.
USA; 1823; purple, yellow, green, and white silk brocade ribbon; 10½" by 2½"

5
Phebe Ann Aylsworth (1791–1829) made this small sampler using only a simple cross stitch. The daughter of Jeremiah and Phebe (Allen) Aylsworth, Phebe Ann lived in North Kingston, Rhode Island. In 1817 she married John Chadsey, with whom she had four children.
North Kingston, R.I.; 1801; off-white linen, embroidered with blue, green, purple, light brown, and black silk; 8" by 5½"

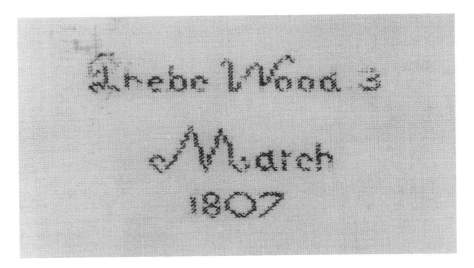

6
This plain homespun handkerchief belonged to Phebe Wood. Because Phebe included the inscription "March 1807," it is possible that she made the handkerchief as part of her trousseau or to commemorate a special occasion. Phebe probably learned her letters by making an embroidered sampler. Note the similarity between these letters and the alphabet in fig. 9.
New England; 1807; off-white linen, embroidered with brown cotton; 25½" by 27"

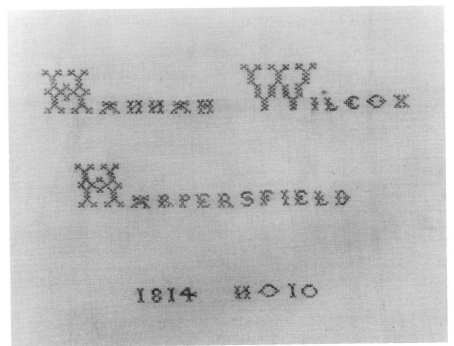

7
On this pillow case, embroidered by Hannah Wilcox in 1814, the "no 10" at the bottom suggests that Hannah made several similar towels, and that this was the tenth in the group. The lettering, although very well stitched, is far more bold than that on Phebe Wood's handkerchief (fig. 6). The letters are similar to those found on Pennsylvania linens, but the pillow case was made across the border in Delaware County, New York.
Detail; Harpersfield, N.Y.; 1814; white linen, embroidered with blue linen; 16" by 36½"

bets and numerals. All stitches were "counted"—that is, spaced according to the warps and wefts of the ground fabric. The stitches ranged in difficulty from the basic cross stitch to star-shaped configurations that required several passes of the needle through the fabric. Lettering, too, ranged in difficulty and style from simple block letters to elaborate script.

A girl learned to embroider letters and numbers because as an adult she would mark her linens with initials, names, dates, and inventory numbers (figs. 6, 7). The necessity for marking possessions dated back to times of community washing areas, when it was important to identify household and personal linens that were otherwise plain and with-

8

Marked linens often became family heirlooms. This is one of a pair of pillow cases handed down through four generations. It bears four cross stitched dates: 1726 (or 1728), 1784, 1812, and 1834. The family, whose last name began with "P," remains unknown but quite possibly lived near New Hope, Pennsylvania, where the cases were purchased.
Detail; Pennsylvania; 1726–1834; off-white linen, embroidered with brown cotton; 17" by 28"

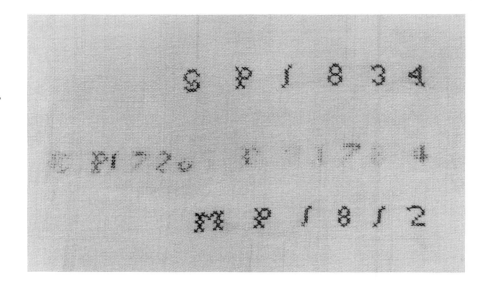

out identifiable characteristics. In the early nineteenth century, not all linens were marked, but those that were followed the earlier conventions. The original function of marking could still be seen in the placement of the initials. Sheets, for example, were often marked with very small letters appearing inconspicuously in one corner. Shirts were marked either on the base of the front opening or on the side seam near the hem. These locations were hidden during normal use, but were visible during cleaning. Although marking became less functional over time, it remained an important tradition. A young woman marked all the linens in her trousseau in anticipation of her wedding day. Marked linens became heirlooms handed down from one generation to the next (fig. 8).

For an intermediate student the formation of letters on samplers became far more than a method of learning how to mark linens. To alphabets and numbers she added short phrases, verses, names, dates, and places (figs. 9, 10). The inscriptions indicate the importance of samplers in the girl's education. By stitching a quotation or a poem, the young embroiderer demonstrated her knowledge of literature, geography, and the Scriptures. The sentiments expressed attested to her grasp of moral principle. Names, dates, and places showed her pride in family and her sense of identity.

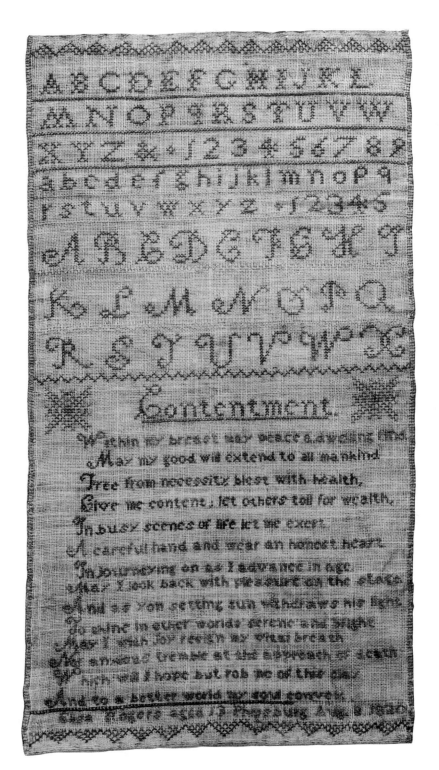

9

Eliza Rogers made this sampler in Phipsburg, Maine, when she was thirteen years old. Eliza, born on 15, June 1807, was the second daughter of Captain George Rogers and Beatrice Mains Rogers. Eliza never married. She lived in Maine until her death in 1865. To complete her sampler, Eliza used cross and buttonhole stitches. The poem, of unknown origin, expresses very typical sentiments of the period and shows that moral teachings were an important part of a young girl's education.

Phipsburg, Maine; 1820; natural linen, embroidered with blue-green, red, and off-white silk; 17″ by 9″ (collection of Pamela Miller Ness and Paul Marc Ness)

10

The Foster family, whose birthdates are recorded on this family record, lived in Billerica, Massachusetts. After the sampler was made, Sally Foster saw the births of five additional siblings. Later in life Sally married James Damon of Reading and took up residence in Ipswich, Massachusetts. Her very typical family register is worked in cross, satin, chain, crewel, and filling stitches. Billerica, Mass.; 1816; natural linen, embroidered with green, white, yellow, and black silk; 19" by 15"

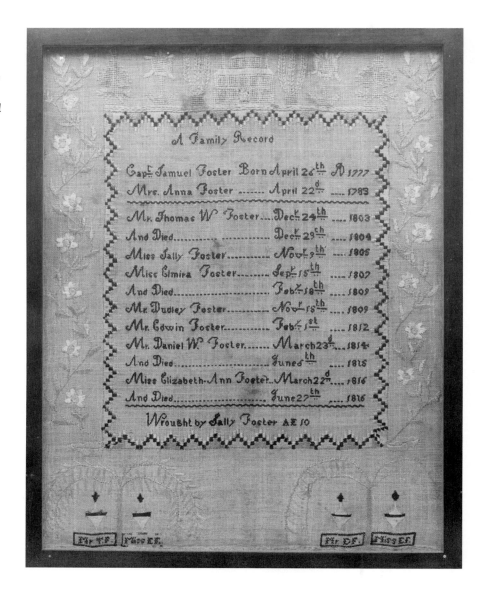

Embroidered Pictures

For an advanced needlework student, the sampler became an ornamental picture. Along with, or in place of, alphabets and words, she embroidered decorative motifs, figures, animals, flowers, or even full scenes (figs. 11, 12). Like inscriptions, these pictorial elements demonstrated the extent of the girl's knowledge. The depiction of realistic flowers indicated that she had studied botany. Biblical symbols showed her religious training. Maps boasted her proficiency in geography.

The use of motifs and pictures in schoolgirl samplers led to an even more elaborate needlework form (figs. 13, 14). Silk embroideries came

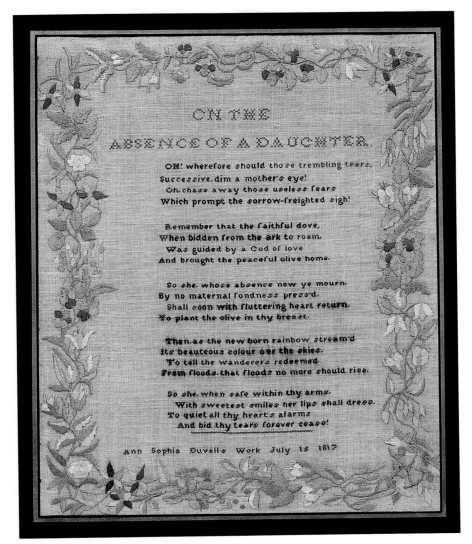

11

Ann Sophia Duvall was the daughter of John Duvall and his second wife, Rebecca Rawlings, whom he married in 1798. Ann Sophia's father was a plantation owner in Ann Arundel County, Maryland. Her sampler was probably made in a Baltimore school, indicated by the distinct floral border rendered in satin stitch. That Ann made the sampler while away from home is suggested by the poem, "On the Absence of a Daughter."

Baltimore, Md.; 1817; natural linen, embroidered in multicolored silk; 21¾″ by 16¾″ (collection of Pamela Miller Ness and Paul Marc Ness)

to American schools from England around 1800. In this art form a picture was drawn or printed on fine white silk fabric, and then covered with silk floss, chenille, and metallic sequins. Portions of the picture, such as the sky, water, and faces, were often painted in. The stitches were difficult to master, and the fine materials made the job laborious. Silk embroideries, therefore, represent the culmination of a girl's needlework training.

Pictorial embroidery also required some artistic training and skill, although a student was not necessarily called upon to draw her own patterns. Rather, these were often supplied by the teacher. The teachers in turn relied heavily on existing prints. The history of silk

12

Mary Ann Catherine Late was born in Frederick, Maryland, the daughter of Michael Late and Ann Maria Hoff Late. Mary Ann came from a German background, yet her sampler reflects little of the German heritage. A Taufschein, a decorative baptismal certificate or announcement, for her father (also in the collection of Professor and Mrs. Edwin Miller) shows the German name "Speth," which indicates that the family was assimilated into Anglo-Saxon culture sometime prior to Mary Ann's birth. In 1832 Mary Ann married William Otis. The couple moved to Rochester, New York, where they raised twelve children. Frederick, Md.; 1824; natural linen, embroidered with multicolored silk and cotton; 21¼" by 19¼"

⁴ I am grateful to Davida Deutsch for sharing some of her unpublished research on Samuel Folwell.

embroideries is entirely correlated with the development of engraving. The most popular teachers had large stores of prints at their disposal. A few teachers employed artists to draw original patterns. Mrs. Folwell's Philadelphia school, for example, benefited from the artistic services of her husband, Samuel, who not only drew the designs, but also painted facial features and inscriptions.⁴

A completed decorative sampler hung on the wall of a girl's home and thus became a part of nineteenth-century interior design. At a time when original paintings were scarce and prints were still expensive, children's artwork was more highly prized than today. (We usually relegate this work to kitchen walls and the refrigerator.) Early nine-

13

This silk embroidery was stitched in about 1800 and modeled after a print entitled "Annette and Luben." The idyllic scene with the shepherdess on a river bank is typical of prints of the 1790s. The unsigned work was probably made in a New England embroidery school. Satin stitches, running stitches, and French knots are used. In customary fashion, the sky, water, faces, hands, and legs are painted directly on the silk satin ground.

Probably New England; ca. 1800; white silk, embroidered with multicolored silk, portions painted; 20¼" by 17½"

teenth-century schoolgirl embroideries were proudly displayed in the parlor, in full view of visiting family and friends. Not only did they stand as the achievement of a talented daughter, but they also testified to the financial and social position of the family, since the materials and the embroidery schooling were both quite costly.

Muslin Work

In addition to plain sewing and silk embroidery, girls learned to apply white cotton thread to a white cotton or linen ground, using a variety of decorative stitches. In the early nineteenth century, all-white

14
Embroidered floral sprays of this type were made in schools in Salem, Massachusetts, in the early nineteenth century. The realistic bouquet of roses, tulips, phlox, carnations, and morning glories is rendered in a satin stitch on an off-white silk satin ground. The girl who made this embroidery exhibited a knowledge of botany. She must also have had some proficiency in the use of watercolors, since a knowledge of painting was considered necessary before attempting works of this type.
Salem, Mass.; ca. 1810; off white satin, embroidered with multicolored silk; 19″ by 14″

embroidery had no distinct name but was referred to generally as "embroidery on muslin"[5] or "working muslin."[6] Today we find it convenient to refer to the style as "muslin work." (Later in the nineteenth century, this work was called "white embroidery" or "white work," names that are still in use.) There were three distinct types of muslin work: embroidery, tambour work, and stuffed work.

The most complex branch of muslin work was embroidery (figs. 15, 16, 17, 18). Within this branch there was an infinite variety of styles and techniques. Historians have attempted to categorize and name the different kinds, using terms like Ayreshire, *Broderie Anglaise*, and Mountmellick. Most of the names refer to geographic locations where

[5] *"Godey's Lady's Book* 1 (1830): 13.

[6] See advertisements for girls' schools quoted in Krueger, *New England Samplers to 1840.*

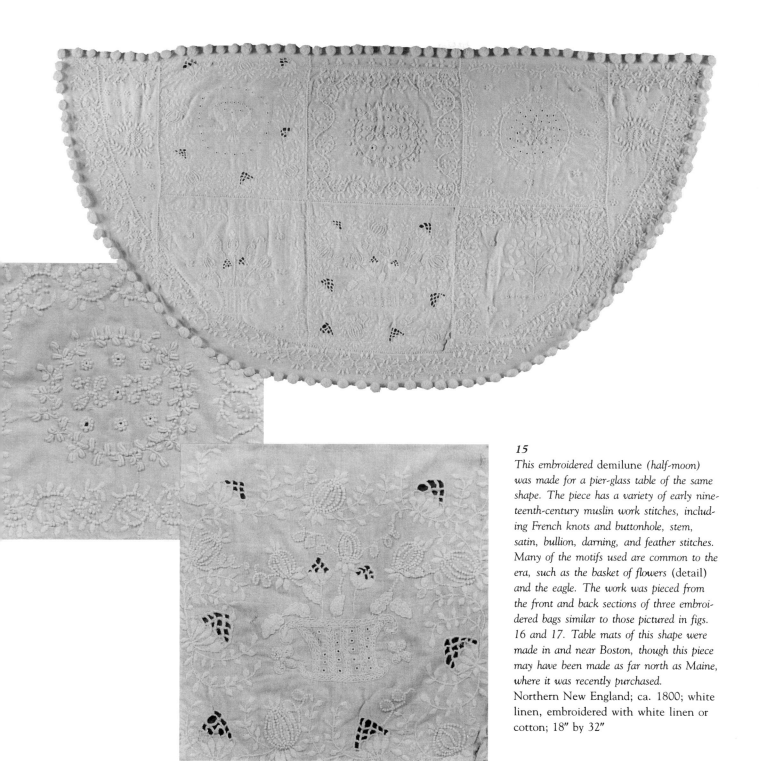

15

This embroidered demilune (half-moon)
was made for a pier-glass table of the same
shape. The piece has a variety of early nineteenth-century muslin work stitches, including French knots and buttonhole, stem,
satin, bullion, darning, and feather stitches.
Many of the motifs used are common to the
era, such as the basket of flowers (detail)
and the eagle. The work was pieced from
the front and back sections of three embroidered bags similar to those pictured in figs.
16 and 17. Table mats of this shape were
made in and near Boston, though this piece
may have been made as far north as Maine,
where it was recently purchased.
Northern New England; ca. 1800; white
linen, embroidered with white linen or
cotton; 18″ by 32″

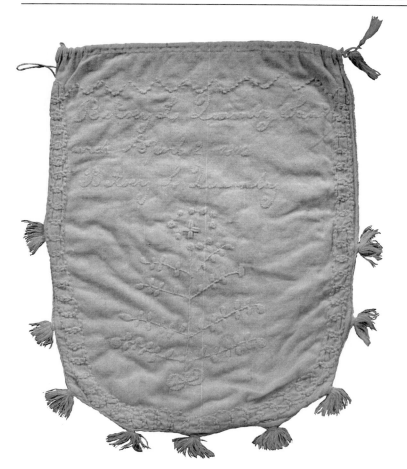

16

Betsey Quinby is probably the Elizabeth Quinby who is recorded as the fourth child of Enoch and Sarah Libby Quinby of Sandwich, New Hampshire. This Betsey (born 1797) would have been eighteen when she made the bag. Perhaps it was worked as part of a class project. Betsey later married a Nathaniel French, also of Sandwich. Sandwich, N.H.; 1816; white cotton, embroidered with white cotton; 10³⁄₄″ by 8¹⁄₂″

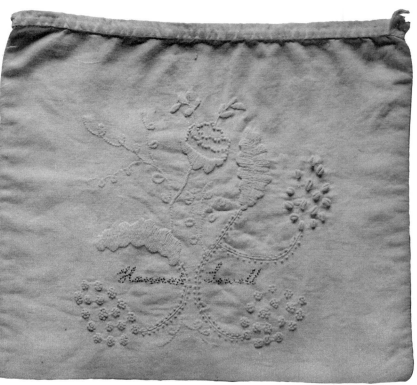

17

Hannah Lowell is far too common a New England name to trace. Her bag, however, is of the same era as Betsey Quinby's and uses many of the same stitches. Small projects like this bag were more frequently the product of domestic embroiderers than were the elegant long cotton dresses for which they served as accessories.

Northern New England; early 19th c.; white cotton, embroidered with white cotton; 7¹⁄₂″ by 8¹⁄₂″

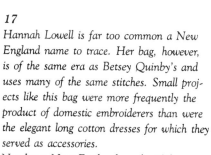

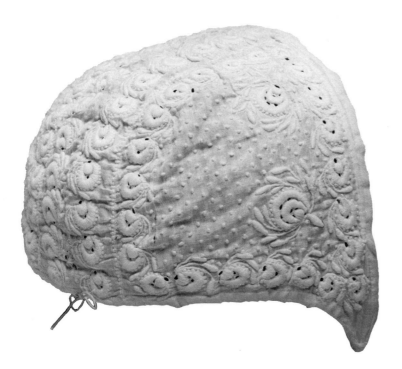

18
In the eighteenth century infants were considered nonhuman, since they could not walk, talk, or think. As more babies survived, both infancy and childhood were recognized as important stages of life. Expectant mothers prepared lavish wardrobes for their infant children. This small baby's cap shows the many delicate muslin work stitches the mother had learned as a youth. USA; early 19th c.; white cotton, embroidered with white cotton; 3½" by 13"

distinct stitches or patterns were common. They identify characteristics that are only vaguely defined and dependent on comparisons with other styles. Ayreshire, for example, is usually finer in texture than *Broderie Anglaise* and has smaller cut-work areas. Mountmellick is usually as heavy as *Broderie Anglaise,* but contains no cut work. Such classifications, formed to describe British embroidery, are less useful to the historian of American works. Many extant muslin work pieces cannot be clearly typed. Evidently, few conventions were precisely followed, and the embroiderer of muslin work was free to use whatever stitches and materials she preferred. Only one kind of embroidered muslin work is sufficiently distinct to be precisely identified. Candlewicking consisted of thick embroidery threads that formed a three-dimensional looped or fringed pile design. Candlewicking developed from similar woven pieces and was primarily used for large bed coverings (fig. 19).

Tambour work, the second form of muslin work, was accomplished with a small hook that pierced the fabric and drew the embroidery thread to the surface in a series of small, interconnected loops, which resembled an embroidered chain stitch. The designs for tambour work frequently used long, continuous lines, since it was difficult to start and stop a chain. Tambour work was not new in the early nineteenth century, nor was it limited to white cotton embroidery threads on a white cotton ground. The suitability of the technique to a wide variety of

19

This white bed covering is decorated with embroidered candlewicking. Note the three-dimensional quality of the work that results from the use of thick embroidery yarns and cut pile threads. Both the central design of a flowering pot and the surrounding vines with clusters of grapes (details) are typical of the era and can be found in many different media of the decorative arts. Note, for example, the similarity between this piece and that shown in fig. 21.

Probably Deerfield, Mass.; 1820; white cotton or linen, embroidered with white cotton; 98½″ by 100½″

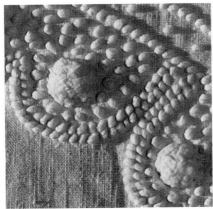

20

Stuffed work, or trapunto, was used for some very beautiful white bed coverings of the early nineteenth century. This piece featured a typical cornucopia motif, surrounded by a wreath of grape clusters. The sculptured quality of white stuffed work would have been particularly effective in bedrooms lit by candles and oil lamps, since their design is seen only through shadows. According to tradition, this spread was made by Harriet Newell Robinson for Martha Wheeler Sibley, and was passed down through the Sibley family.
Detail; Randolph Center, Vt.; ca. 1811; white cotton, quilted with cotton thread; 72" by 82"

materials, as well as the ease with which the stitch could be mastered, probably accounted for the great popularity of tambour work.

Stuffed work, the third form of muslin work, refers to objects that were either quilted or corded (figs. 20, 21). In this branch of muslin work, two layers of fabric were bound together with a running stitch that was both functional and decorative. Between the two layers was placed padding or cording, which either extended across the entire width of the piece or was concentrated in specific areas. The padding and the stitching resulted in a three dimensional design, which was apparent only when the work was indirectly lit. White stuffed work was used for petticoats, corsets, large bed coverings, and table mats. Like tambour work, stuffed work was not restricted to white threads on white muslin.

Muslin Work Designs

As she had when she was a schoolgirl, a woman generally relied on others to supply her with patterns for muslin work. Often she took her linen to be marked by an artist, purchased hand-drawn designs at a fancy shop,[7] or took a pattern from an existing piece of needlework by placing a piece of paper over the embroidery and rubbing the surface with nutmeg.[8] There were a few published pattern books for muslin

[7] See, for example, those reproduced in Mildred J. Davis, *Embroidery Designs, 1780–1820: From the Manuscript Collection of the Textiles Resource and Research Center of the Valentine Museum* (New York: Crown Publishers, 1971).

[8] *Godey's Lady's Book* 1 (1830): 13.

work, but most of them were printed in Germany. The quantity and the complexity of the patterns in the German publications suggest that they were intended for professional embroiderers or for the proprietors of fancy shops. Most patterns, whether published or drawn, appear only as line drawings, so that the craftswoman needed considerable skill in both composition and embroidery to turn out a masterpiece.

All-white needlework in its various forms would never have become so important had it not fitted in with the aesthetic taste of the era. Beginning in the 1780s women had begun to shed their silk gowns in favor of white cotton high-waisted frocks. Architecture and interior design saw a similar simplification of line and an interest in the color white. The new shapes of the late eighteenth and early nineteenth centuries required subtle surface decorations, which were adequately achieved through white on white embroidery. The designs used in muslin work closely follow those found in other decorative arts. Classical art inspired the greatest number of designs: cornucopias abound, as do urns and garlands of flowers.

In addition to classical motifs, eagles and other patriotic symbols are found on both children's and adults' work. These reflected the trend toward a single national identity. At the same time, the country's separate geographic regions retained some stylistic differences. The geographic styles can be organized by the major cities, for most small

21

This table mat, made for a semicircular table, is composed of two layers of cotton, which are quilted. Stuffing has been added in the design areas to give the piece a three-dimensional quality. The maker, Ruth Cloyes, was the daughter of John and Desire Perry Cloyes, who lived in Haverhill, Massachusetts. At about the time this piece was made, Ruth married a William Gleason and moved to Barnet, Vermont. Ruth can be identified because she is the only Ruth Cloyes who spelled her maiden name with an "o" (rather than an "a"); She even named her fourth son Cloyes W. Gleason. Haverhill, Mass.; 1799–1800; white cotton, quilted with white cotton; 15" by 33¾"

towns along the east coast fell within the sphere of influence of Boston, New York, Philadelphia, Baltimore, Washington, or Richmond. Small white handbags and table mats in a half-moon shape, for example, seem to have been most popular in and around Boston. Further stylistic differences can be attributed to specific teachers or pattern designers, each of whom influenced the designs and techniques used by the domestic embroiderer.

The Function of Muslin Work

If samplers and silk embroidery were the most common products of childhood sewing, muslin work was the most common fancy work made by women. Muslin work was widely used simply because most of the garments and household linens traditionally made in the home were white, and women were more likely to embellish items they had made than those they had purchased. Baby clothing, caps, petticoats, table mats, and bed coverings provided perfect surfaces to decorate. Because items would eventually wear out and need replacing, a woman would be able to continue embroidering muslin work her entire life.

Muslin work suited the democratic ideals and the pocketbooks of early nineteenth-century Americans. Not only did the designs hark back to ancient times, but the materials were available to a wide segment of the population. Most silk was imported and quite costly, as were many dyes, such as indigo. Silk was tricky to work with and difficult to keep clean. On the other hand, muslin and linen were available in many grades to suit a variety of budgets. The materials were relatively easy to work with. If left white, muslin and linen were long-lasting and could not fade. Muslin work was, of course, decorative embroidery and took skill, money, and time. But in contrast to silk embroidery and samplers, white on white embroidery was found in the homes of middle- and upper-class women alike, in cities, small towns, and even the sparsely populated countryside.

*The
Early
Victorian
Period*

1830–1860

When the Englishwoman Fanny Trollope visited the United States in 1829–1830, she found a country of 12 million people spread throughout the area east of the Mississippi, but still concentrated along the eastern seaboard. She traveled, although not easily or comfortably, from New Orleans to Cincinnati, and from Baltimore to Niagara Falls. The people she met along the way were small farmers, land owners, shopkeepers, and members of urban high society. She saw both the extremely poor and the very wealthy. People had an interest in and a knowledge of art and philosophy and were far more educated and sophisticated than she had expected.

During the 30 years following Mrs. Trollope's visit, the nation would see great changes. By 1860 the population would again double in size and would spread far west of the Mississippi. Train travel became commonplace, and with increased rail service came improvements in communication. New technological developments brought a wider range and a greater quantity of American-made goods to all citizens. Concurrent with the development of industry was the growth of cities, and thus the formation of distinct urban and rural lifestyles.

Apart from physical changes, the country would be affected by three important movements. From Germany came a new style of artistic expression now called Biedermeier, which combined the ideas of Romantic and Realistic painting and idealized middle-class life. From

England came Victorian morality (Victoria became queen in 1837) and an emphasis on a tight family unit with a very rigid set of duties for women. And throughout the country Americans witnessed the growth of evangelicalism as well as the popularization of such secular causes as temperance and abolitionism. These three forces would affect women's activities and women's artwork.

With the new era came new materials, techniques, and designs for America's needleworkers. German wools, glass beads, and human hair replaced the fine silk floss and cotton embroidery threads of the previous years. Both soft and bright colors supplanted the classically inspired white. Simple, evenly arranged, counted stitches were favored over the numerous freely drawn stitches of muslin work and silk embroidery. The subject matter grew more sentimental, more ornate, more Victorian.

Canvas Work

Undoubtedly the most popular form of pictorial embroidery in mid-nineteenth-century America was canvas work (fig. 22). In its technique canvas work was related to sampler making, since it employed counted stitches, such as the cross stitch. Unlike samplers, however, canvas work usually involved covering the entire ground fabric with embroidery thread. It resembled silk embroidery in portraying realistic flowers, animals, birds, or complete scenes. Rather than silk, however, canvas work primarily employed German wool, popularly termed "Berlin wool." It therefore was called (correctly) "Berlin wool work," or (less correctly) "Berlin work." Both terms were introduced well into the history of the craft, replacing a large number of less clear names. For example, *Godey's Lady's Book* of 1830 described the technique, calling it variously "pictorial" or "coloured embroidery" and "worsted work."[1] And because the finished piece resembled tapestry, it was sometimes referred to as "tapestry work."

Technically, canvas work was ideally suited to the capabilities of American women. After 1830 American girls received far less needlework training than had their mothers and grandmothers. Schools and curricula were changing. In the private schools, needlework became an extracurricular activity, one that required a small fee in addition to tuition and room and board. As public schools were established, a larger number of girls received a basic education. However, "basic" most frequently meant studying the humanities. Where needlework was included, the emphasis was on plain sewing, not fancy embroidery. For girls who reached their majority without knowing how to embroider, canvas work was easily learned. There were many stitches from which

[1] *Godey's Lady's Book* 1 (1830): 156, 200.

22

The sampler, made by Margaret Briner, is a transitional piece, for although it follows the form of traditional schoolgirl samplers, it employs the techniques of Berlin wool work. The motifs are all found in imported pattern books and are cross stitched in wool. Note the interest in realistically portrayed flowers, whether bouquets, garlands, or wreaths. The embroiderer was the daughter of Jacob Briner of Reading, Pennsylvania. In 1843 she married Daniel Wieland, also of Reading.

Reading, Pa.; 1839; natural linen, embroidered with multicolored wool and brown cotton; 17¼″ by 18¼″

to choose, but only a handful were widely used, and it was possible to work a remarkable piece after mastering only one stitch.

Of course, the embroiderers of canvas work did not perceive their task as easy. The selection of materials was large, and the choices that faced the needleworker were many. She had to choose the proper type of canvas, a needle of the right size, and the appropriate wool embroidery threads. She had to stretch the canvas on a frame, select and master the type of stitch to be used, and begin in the correct corner of the work. The most difficult phase seems to have been the grounding (putting the threads in a large monochromatic background area), which was often done badly (fig. 23).

Canvas Work Designs

Like the counted-thread wool work of previous centuries, canvas work satisfied two purposes. The first was to provide a surface decoration for a functional object. Projects in this category ranged in size from tiny needle cases to chair seats to area rugs. Canvas work adorned sewing tools (pincushions and sewing boxes), furnishings (wall pockets and book covers; fig. 24), upholstery (chairs and footstools), and clothing (suspenders and vests). The variety of objects was remarkable. As

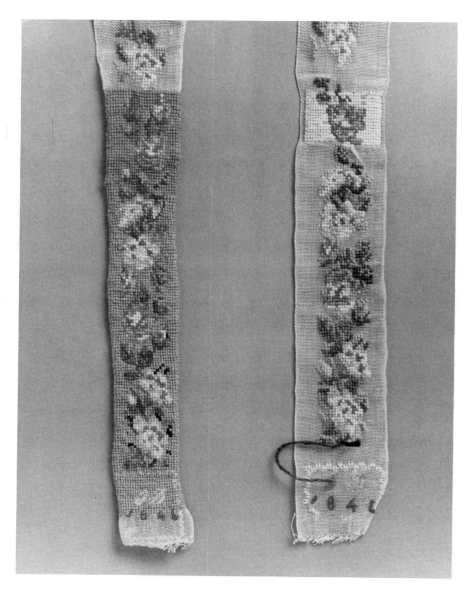

23

Canvas work suspenders were considered appropriate gifts for a father, husband or brother. This pair of unfinished suspenders clearly illustrates the materials and methods used in Berlin work. The plain woven canvas was sold in narrow strips. Floral motifs were worked first, with the background, or grounding, added later. The fact that many women found grounding both tedious and difficult may explain why this pair remains unfinished and why various parts of the ground use wool of different colors.

Pennsylvania; 1841; natural linen, embroidered with multicolored wool; 24″ by 2″

24

The small motifs seen in Margaret Briner's sampler (fig. 22) were also designed to adorn small objects, such as this notebook, which could easily be carried in a woman's pocket. The shrine surrounded by trees was a popular design. An equally well known design, a bowl with doves, appears on the reverse.

USA; mid 19th c.; off-white linen, embroidered with multicolored silk; 5¹/₈″ by 3¹/₂″

25

Bell-pulls were both a functional item and a status symbol, since they not only allowed a family to call their servant, but told visitors quite plainly that there were servants to call. That bell-pulls were frequently rendered in canvas work indicates the status of the craft as well. In the middle of the century, Berlin wool work was prominently displayed in many middle- and upper-middle-class homes. This was not the case in the latter part of the century, when the craft became less fashionable.

USA; mid 19th c.; light brown silk canvas, embroidered with red, yellow, brown, and green silk and wool; 81″ by 4¼″

26

The flowers in early Berlin patterns, though depicted by a series of small squares, appear to be quite realistic. The overall shape of this pattern suggests that it was designed as a chair back. It bears the name of Carl F. W. Wicht, a well-known printer, who worked in Berlin between 1838 and 1858.

Berlin, Germany; ca. 1850; paper, printed and painted; 23″ by 17½″

27

Canvas work not only decorated functional objects, but also appeared in framed pictures used to adorn walls. This tiny still life shows a remarkable sensitivity to color and shading and is reminiscent of similar paintings of the era. Because silk embroidery threads remained costly, they were used only for very small works, or as highlights in larger pictures.
New Jersey; ca. 1840; off-white silk, embroidered with multicolored silk; 4″ by 5″

Godey's stated in 1830, canvas work was suitable for "rugs for urns, covers of ottomans, bell-pulls, and many other elegant articles" (fig. 25).[2] When canvas work decorated a functional object, the design was most likely floral (fig. 26), with birds, animals, and the like as secondary motifs. The rendering of these objects was always as realistic as possible, given the scale of the work and the fact that it was done within a grid pattern.

Framed pictures, made to hang on walls, constituted a second category of Berlin work. Pictures ranged in size from about 2 by 3 inches to roughly 2 by 3 feet (compare figs. 27 and 28). The small pictures generally contained a single motif, such as a horse, while the larger works frequently included several figures or full scenes. Since they were intended as wall decorations, the pictures copied popular prints and drawings. There is no question that these pictorial works resemble the genre scenes of the Biedermeier painters and the subsequent Realists. The resemblance to German painting styles can be attributed to the fact that many patterns for canvas work were manufactured in Germany or Austria.

Despite the German origin of most of the materials and patterns, however, Berlin wool work became an international needlecraft. Printers in Berlin and other cities catered to the tastes of their international market. Rustic scenes were inspired by the interest in national

[2] *Godey's Lady's Book* 2 (1831): 25.

28

The peasant scene in this canvas work picture reflects the new interest in European ethnic traditions that accompanied the spread of nationalistic movements on the continent. Note the traditional dress worn by the man smoking the pipe. The idealized family is also typical of the interior genre pictures of the Biedermeier painters. The design, called "Family Happiness," was published by Z. A. Grünthal, who worked in Berlin from 1834 to 1862.
New Jersey; ca. 1850–1860; off-white cotton, embroidered with multicolored wool; 22½″ by 19½″

dress and local customs that was spreading throughout Europe (fig. 28). Peacocks, King Charles spaniels, and historical scenes from Britain's past were produced for export to England (fig. 29). For America, the German publishers manufactured portraits of George Washington and Abraham Lincoln as well as scenes from popular American novels like *Uncle Tom's Cabin* (fig. 30).

29

Popular Berlin patterns copied famous paintings. The source for this one, "Charles the first after parting with his children," was probably one or more paintings by Anton Van Dyck, a Flemish painter of the seventeenth century. The pattern was made for the English market by the Berlin printer Z. A. Grünthal, the same firm that produced the pattern called "Family Happiness" (see fig. 28).
Berlin, Germany; 1850–1860; paper, printed and painted; 29″ by 20″

Charles the first after parting with his children.

30

According to the legend on the reverse of this work, the picture was embroidered by Jessie Gorris in 1858 and 1859. It took Jessie four months to complete it. The scene is from Harriet Beecher Stowe's Uncle Tom's Cabin, which was published in 1853. The book became an overnight bestseller, translated into many languages. Most editions of the book included an illustration entitled "Uncle Tom and Eva." This rendition may have come directly from one of the German editions, or may have been especially designed for the unidentified publisher of the pattern.

USA; 1859; off-white cotton, embroidered with multicolored wool; 26″ by 21″

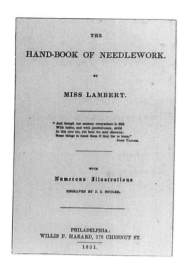

31

Miss Lambert, an English author, thanked her husband for allowing her to use her own name, a tribute to her remarkable talents and popularity. Her Hand-Book of Needlework appeared in 1842. An American edition was available in the same year; the German translation appeared as early as 1846. Probably the most widely known needlework book of the era, it was still being reprinted as late as 1854.

³ Miss Lambert, *The Hand-Book of Needlework: Decorative and Ornamental, Including Crochet, Knitting and Netting*, 4th ed. (New York: Wiley and Putnam, 1842), 15.

⁴ Needlework was hardly the only subject to benefit from the improved technologies that swept through the bookmaking industry after 1830. Other books for women included etiquette manuals, cook books, and works on domestic economy.

⁵ *Die Allzeit fertige Stickerin, ein Geschenk für das schöne Geschlecht, oder, Anweisung, wie eine Stickerin sich selbst, ohne zeichnen zu können, jedes Muster ab- und auf-zeichnen und fortfuhren kann*, 2d ed. (Meissen: F. W. Goedsche, ca. 1825).

Berlin Patterns

What distinguished the new Berlin work from seventeenth- and eighteenth-century canvas work were the patterns printed on "point paper," which resembled graph paper. Each square represented a crossing of the warp and weft on the ground fabric. Within the squares a printed code indicated the color of thread to be stitched in that location. Common codes were dots, slashes, crescents, and combinations thereof. Inexpensive patterns printed in a single color were sold, but more elaborate patterns were meticulously hand painted or printed in the correct shades.

Berlin patterns were developed by German printers in the early years of the nineteenth century. Although the beginning of the technology has been cloaked in a charming story of a single printer and his wife, in fact the two components of Berlin patterns were well established by 1800. In the first place, the configuration of the patterns—that is, the coded graph—had been used for some time to indicate weaving patterns. Second, German printers were already manufacturing patterns for other types of embroidery, and in particular for muslin work, called *weisse Stickerei* or "white embroidery." Combining the two traditions was a logical step.

Because the great majority of embroiderers relied on commercially produced patterns, successful canvas work did not require an ability to draw or paint. The embroiderer had only to count properly and correctly place her stitches. Even the correct color scheme was indicated on each pattern, further limiting the need for artistic decisions. But not all embroiderers held hand-colored patterns in high regard. Miss Lambert, speaking for the embroiderers, thought that the makers of German patterns used "neither taste nor judgment . . . in the selection of colors" and believed the finished product of the needlewoman was always far superior.³ Another writer cautioned women who were reproducing actual paintings to view the original work, since the pattern colorist often chose the wrong shades.

Needlework Manuals

Regardless of how easy canvas work appeared, embroiderers needed some instruction and an explanation of materials, terminology, and stitches. As fewer embroidery classes were available, their place was taken by printed how-to manuals and periodicals.⁴ An early lead in the production of embroidery manuals had been taken by German printers, for in addition to patterns and pattern books, publishers from 1795 to 1830 offered directions for all kinds of needlework, "so that an embroiderer can copy and follow a pattern, without being able to draw."⁵

32
These small books, published as a series in New York by J. S. Redfield, were among the few needlework manuals printed in the United States in the 1840s. The anonymous editor signed herself "An American Lady," an indication that writing books was not yet considered a respectable occupation for women. The books were available as a set or separately. They cover the full range of needlework produced in the 1840s, including both plain and fancy work.

After 1830 production of manuals spread to France, England, and America.

English-language manuals of 1830 to 1860 were written largely by British women. Some were printed in small quantities and distributed almost exclusively in Britain. For example, Savage's *Winchester Fancy Needlework Instructor* was dedicated "To the Ladies of the United Kingdom" and had a printing of only 6,000 volumes.[6] More often, however, the manuals reached a wider audience. Warren and Pullan's *Treasures in Needlework* was written for "Lady Needleworkers throughout the world"[7] and was exported to the United States. British books were regularly reprinted by American publishers. The most popular of these was Miss Lambert's *Hand-Book of Needlework* (1842), which went through several printings in New York and Philadelphia in addition to the original London editions (fig. 31).

Because copyright laws were in their infancy, the American editions did not always give credit to the original sources. Some did so casually; the *Lady's Work-Box Companion*, compiled by "A Lady of New York," was actually "revised and enlarged" from "the latest London edition."[8] These instances of plagiarism prove two points. First, the market for instructional manuals was large. Second, the difference between the styles or techniques of England and America was insignificant. Occasionally American publishers "corrected" the English spellings or added new material, but by and large they reprinted English patterns and instructions verbatim.

Two works were written by American women during this era. The first was actually a series of small books edited anonymously and published by J. S. Redfield in 1843[9] (fig. 32). The second was a substantial volume written by Florence Hartley in 1859.[10] The two publications

[6] Mrs. William Savage, *The Winchester Fancy Needlework Instructor and Manual of the Fashionable and Elegant Accomplishment of Knitting and Crochet*, 3d ed. (London: Simpkin, Marshall & Co., [1847]).

[7] Mrs. E. Warren and Mrs. M. M. Pullan, *Treasures in Needlework: Comprising Instructions in Knitting, Netting, Crochet, Point Lace, Tatting, Braiding, and Embroidery* (London: Ward & Lock, 1855).

[8] *The Lady's Work-Box Companion: Being Instructions in All Varieties of Canvas Work, with Twenty-nine Engraved Specimens* (New York: Burgess, Stringer, & Co., 1844).

[9] The "Ladies Handbook" series; for individual volumes, see Appendix, Part 2.

[10] Florence Hartley, *The Ladies Hand-Book of Fancy and Ornamental Work, Comprising Directions and Patterns for Working in Appliqué, Bead Work, Braiding, Canvas Work, Knitting, Netting, Tatting, Worsted Work, Quilting, Patchwork, &c., &c.* (Philadelphia: G. G. Evans, 1859).

33

Because Queen Victoria owned a King Charles spaniel, a number of very similar Berlin patterns depicted this breed of dog sitting regally on an overstuffed cushion. In this example, the hair of the animal is worked in the plush stitch, which is untrimmed except around the face and paws. The dog and pillow are worked on canvas that has been cut out and appliquéd to black velvet, a common technique used in order to avoid grounding a large area. New England; ca. 1850–1860; canvas embroidered with multicolored silk and wool, black velvet ground; 19³/₄″ by 23³/₄″

[11] *Godey's Lady's Book* 33 (1846): 43.

illustrate the major changes that took place in sewing manuals of this era. The Redfield books cover a variety of subjects, many of them practical. Plain needlework, millinery and dressmaking, and baby linen, for example, accounted for three of the six volumes. Pictures, still expensive to produce, were kept to a minimum. By Hartley's era, not only had the number and quality of drawings improved, but the subject matter was far more decorative than practical.

Instructional manuals were supplemented by articles on needlework, which appeared in nearly every woman's magazine of the 1830–1860 period. *Godey's Lady's Book*, for example, included embroidery patterns and instructions in its first issues (beginning in 1830). Again, the purpose of the articles was clearly educational. *Godey's* launched its new "Ladies Work Department" in 1846, "intending to present to the ladies who honor us with their favor a series of drawings and descriptions which will enable those who wish, to take up these new kinds of needlework without a teacher."[11]

Canvas Work Variations

The popularity of Berlin patterns can be explained partially by their great versatility. Slight variations could be achieved by using new stitches, such as the raised stitches of plushwork. Plushwork was very similar in technique to canvas work, starting with the same canvas ground. It also resembled candlewicking and rug hooking in that the embroidery stitch came away from the ground to form a pile. If rendered with long threads, either cut or uncut, the pile could resemble the fur of an animal (fig. 33). If the threads were cut short, the needleworker could form three-dimensional flowers (fig. 34).

Berlin patterns were also worked in materials other than wool. For example, beads could be woven together or sewn on canvas in the

34

The flowers that form the wreath in this plushwork embroidery are the same ones found in many Berlin patterns. In this piece, the use of the plush stitch has allowed the embroiderer to achieve a three-dimensional effect. The loops of the pile have been sheared to make the flowers appear round Ithaca, N.Y.; mid 19th c.; 16½″ by 15½″

35

Beads were added as highlights to many Berlin wool work embroideries. In this small picture, beads form the flower design, and wool threads are limited to the ground. The shiny texture and the white, gray, and black tones of the flowers are accented against the dark red wool background
USA; mid 19th c.; canvas embroidered with red wool and white, gray, and black glass beads; 6¾″ by 9″

36

Berlin work patterns could be easily adapted to beadwork by using one bead for every painted square. Glass beads were heavy, so most beadwork projects remained small. Small Berlin work patterns were particularly suitable for purses, such as this example signed by E. Greyble and dated "March 10, 1835." The bag was probably made in Pennsylvania, which (according to 1830 and 1840 census reports) had the largest number of Greyble family members.
Pennsylvania; 1835; multicolored glass beads with red-purple silk top [top may be a later addition]; 5″ by 2¾″

37

An essential tool in every sewing kit was a small needle case used to store both pins and needles. The variety of decorations on needle cases and pincushions of the mid nineteenth century is remarkable. This example is worked in beadwork, and a very common wreath pattern surrounds the date (1834). On the reverse is a large rose surrounded by leaves and small flowers. Note the unusual shape, complemented by the stuffed strawberries hanging from the end. Small objects such as this were used as gifts or contributions to fancy fairs.
Possibly Pennsylvania; 1834; off-white and light blue silk, off-white wool, paper, and multicolored glass beads;
2½″ by 2½″

exact configuration of a Berlin pattern (fig. 35). The use of glass beads was not new in 1830. During the late eighteenth and early nineteenth centuries, beadwork had been taught in certain schools as a form of fancy work. Around 1830 beadwork became a craft of the middle classes. Beads were more durable than the wool yarns and provided a shiny texture. But beadwork was difficult to accomplish (it was easy to break the beads through rough handling or by using the wrong needle), and the finished product was very heavy. The work is therefore generally limited to very small artifacts. Cushions, small bags, wrist bands, belts, and pictures made at this time followed Berlin patterns (figs. 36, 37).

Similarly, Berlin patterns were suitable for working in wool on punched paper. In this variation, a piece of stiff paper or cardboard perforated with evenly spaced holes replaced the cloth ground. The embroiderer added diagonal or cross stitches between the holes. Probably the most common use of perforated work was for bookmarks, a use prompted by the concurrent increase in the availability of printed material (figs. 38, 39). Once the fad for bookmarks spread, patternmakers supplied designs specifically for this purpose, including a variety of small motifs such as crosses and anchors, and mottoes like "Holy Bible," "forget me not," and "temperance." These small tokens were sometimes created by children and were considered a suitable present for a relative or friend. They frequently expressed the moral and religious sentiments of the era.

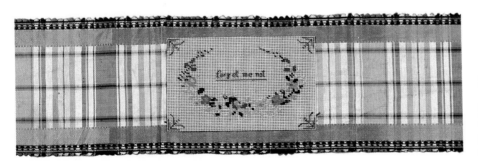

38
The use of bookmarks accompanied the increased production of books in the 1840s. Many were worked in silk or wool on perforated cards following small Berlin patterns. Often used as small gifts or tokens of affection, bookmarks display sentiments related to friendship. This marker, inscribed "forget me not," shows a wreath of flowers from a popular Berlin pattern. The card is mounted on a plaid ribbon typical of the 1850s.
USA; ca. 1850–1860; punched paper, embroidered with multicolored silk and wool, mounted on predominantly pink and white plaid silk ribbon; 15½" by 3¾"

39

In addition to promoting friendship, bookmarks contained religious and memorial inscriptions. This example was made to commemorate Anna Kitchel, who died on June 1, 1858. Like the memorial pictures of the first decades of the century, it features a monument surrounded by plants. Tucked in behind the memorial stone are two small locks of hair, which presumably belonged to Anna.

USA; 1858; punched paper, embroidered with white, gray and green wool and hair, mounted on an off-white silk ribbon; 10″ by 3¹/₄″

40

Punched paper work was also used for a variety of small boxes, pouches, and wall pockets. The pocket on which this design appears contains a printed copy of the poem "Farewell to St. Joseph's," written by Miss Abby Meaher in 1848. Presumably the pocket was worked by a graduating student of Mother Seton's well-known Baltimore school. This piece was worked in silk chenille threads, which, in addition to being more expensive than wool, give the pocket a rich, plush appearance.

Baltimore, Md.; ca. 1848; punched paper, embroidered with silk chenille, lined with off-white silk and trimmed with gold foil and off-white silk tassels; 10³/₄″ by 12¹/₂″

Throughout the middle of the century, the use of punched paper increased, as did the size of the projects. Sewing boxes, envelopes, decorative pictures, and samplers were all worked in Berlin wools on perforated paper (figs. 40, 41). The technique had definite merit; the board offered a background that did not have to be covered with wool, saving both time and money. In addition, the sturdy board required no stretcher, as was necessary with canvas grounds. However, perforated paper work carried the same disadvantages as beadwork. Many embroiderers used a needle that was too thick, causing the paper to rip. And unless the perforated board was extremely thick, with large holes, only small-scale artifacts were practical.

Despite its enormous popularity, canvas work and its several variations did not constitute the sole needlework output of American women in the early Victorian period. A few forms known before 1830 (such as silk embroidery and stuffed work) had virtually disappeared, and other forms (samplers and tambour work) became less prevalent. But plain sewing, muslin work, and marking remained in use after 1830, albeit with certain stylistic changes. And to these familiar crafts were added embroidered net and crochet.

41
The cross and book motif, very popular on bookmarks, is here used in series to document this embroiderer's extended family. Each cross is marked with a husband's and wife's name. The branches coming from the base of the cross signify children. That this piece records a specific family is underscored by the use of human hair, which was seen as an everlasting part of a person. The crosses are worked in hair, and circlets of hair form the flowers.
Maine; ca. 1850–1860; punched paper, embroidered with multicolored silk and hair; 7″ by 8½″

42

Plain sewing stitches were all that was required to make this small gingham needle case. It was sewn by an ancestor of Cordelia Ball, who lived in Fairhaven, Vermont. Fairhaven, Vt.; mid-19th c.; multicolored cotton prints and blue, tan, and black wool; 9″ by 3¹/₄″

43

Prior to the mid-nineteenth century, ladies' dresses had a slit in the seam but no attached pocket. Pockets like this were worn under the skirt and tied around the waist. They were made of calico scraps or of white linen, like this one, and were among the personal linens on which a woman used her plain sewing skills. New England; ca. 1830; white linen and twill tape; 15″ by 13³/₄″

Plain Sewing

Sewing machines were not yet available to the home sewer at a reasonable price or in sufficient quantity to have a strong impact on plain sewing. The practical stitches used to sew seams, hems, and buttonholes were still the first a girl learned and the ones that she would use most frequently throughout her life. She did not have any other way of making the household and personal linens needed by her family (figs. 42–44). As the pace of life quickened, however, there were indications that women considered plain sewing tedious. The heroines of Louisa May Alcott's *Little Women*, who spend much of the novel sewing or knitting, are honest about it. Meg, who would become the

44
In the first years of the nineteenth century, heavily boned stays were replaced by relatively comfortable corsets, unboned except for a wide ivory or wood "busk" inserted in the center front casing. Stiffness was added through cording sewn between the two layers of fabric. Tight straps held the shoulders as far back as possible. These corsets laced up the back, which meant that a woman had to be dressed by someone else. However, because they were of simple cut and construction, women were no longer wholly dependent on professional corset-makers. And because the corsets were unboned, they could be decorated with embroidery. New Hampshire; ca. 1830; white cotton, embroidered with gold silk; 18" by 10¼"

45

This white embroidered coverlet bears the date 1854 but resembles the fashionable muslin work spreads of earlier decades. Note the cornucopia in the center and the surrounding vines with grape clusters, flowers, and leaves. Note also the knotted fringe along the border. That such an old-fashioned style persisted in mid-century may be explained by the remote location where the coverlet was made or by the ages of the makers. The design and technique prove that this coverlet was made in two stages or by two women. Perhaps the central area was the work of Betsy Webster, while the borders and a portion of the fringe were the work of Sismantha Johnson.

New Hampshire; 1854; white cotton, embroidered with white cotton; 94½" by 98" epitome of the Victorian wife and mother, says, "I'll make the shirts for Father. . . . I can and I will, though I'm not fond of sewing."[12] Tomboy Jo comes up with a way to make sewing sheets more interesting. The girls "adopted Jo's plan of dividing the long seams into four parts, and calling the quarters Europe, Asia, Africa, and America, and in that way got on capitally, especially when they talked about the different countries as they stitched their way through them."[13]

Muslin Work and Marking

Both muslin work and marking survived through the 1830–1860 era, but with some changes. In muslin work, the primary change involved quantity and proportion. A few large-scale works, such as coverlets, can be dated to the mid-century, but these are rendered in basic stitches (fig. 45). The projects illustrated in magazines and manuals appear to be relatively simple, and few attempts were made to explain the stitches. Evidently, to embroider the corner of a handkerchief or a very narrow collar was now considered a major undertaking (figs. 46, 47).

The scale of projects was not limited merely by the abilities of the mid-century needlewomen; it also depended on the evolution of taste and fashion. Well-dressed women in the beginning of the century had worn elaborately embroidered muslin dresses and silk gowns topped with a wide embroidered muslin collar. But in the 1830s the wide bertha collar became a modest band of embroidered muslin or lace. Similarly, interior design emphasized stronger colors with fewer white surfaces. That the amount of professionally made muslin work also declined in this period further suggests that the trend was related more to fashion than to the abilities of housewives.

Marking continued as a custom, though with a much altered look; a full first name or large initial was embroidered in fancy script, using not counted-thread work, but the stitches of muslin work. Each issue of *Godey's Lady's Book* offered patterns for the more common names, such as Amelia, Caroline, and Amanda. Similar magazines offered elaborately drawn alphabets that often included the most popular motifs of the day. Unlike those used early in the century, the new letters were quite large and complex. It was during this era that the term "monogram" was introduced. That they were no longer practical in nature is evidenced by the illegibility of the letters, conspicuously placed but often camouflaged by a sea of flowers and scrolling lines.

[12] Louisa May Alcott, *Little Women* (1868–1869; reprinted ed., New York and Scarborough, Ontario: New American Library, 1983), 111. Although this novel was written in 1868–1869 and although the plot begins in 1861, it is based on the childhood memories of Alcott, who was born in 1832.

[13] Ibid., 11.

46

When used as a decoration for clothing, muslin work of the middle part of the century appeared primarily on objects of modest size. This narrow collar of white cotton embroidered on muslin mimics professionally made lace. Note, for example, the repeated leaves, the scalloped shape, the looped edge, and the small flowers near the neck. All these are commonly found in the laces of the era.

Near Boston, Mass.; mid-19th c.; white cotton, embroidered with white cotton; 3½" by 14½"

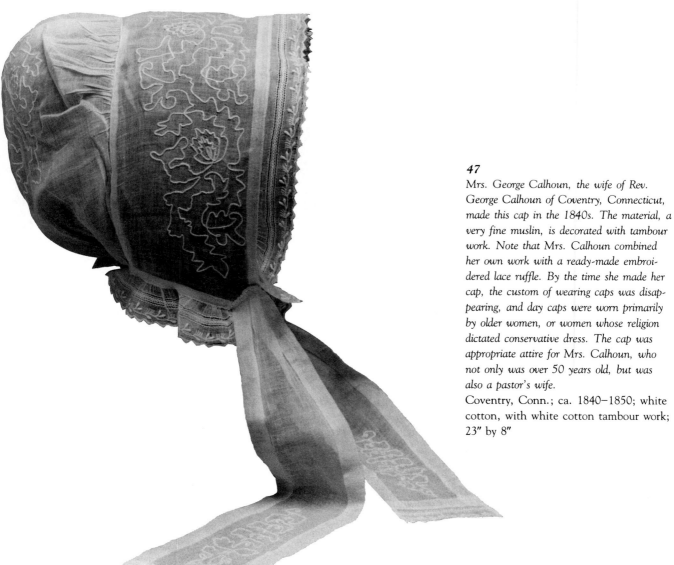

47

Mrs. George Calhoun, the wife of Rev. George Calhoun of Coventry, Connecticut, made this cap in the 1840s. The material, a very fine muslin, is decorated with tambour work. Note that Mrs. Calhoun combined her own work with a ready-made embroidered lace ruffle. By the time she made her cap, the custom of wearing caps was disappearing, and day caps were worn primarily by older women, or women whose religion dictated conservative dress. The cap was appropriate attire for Mrs. Calhoun, who not only was over 50 years old, but was also a pastor's wife.

Coventry, Conn.; ca. 1840–1850; white cotton, with white cotton tambour work; 23" by 8"

48
"Real" lace referred to that which was hand made with a needle or with bobbins. The European real lace industry grew in the mid-century, but the craft was far too tedious and difficult for most domestic embroiderers to handle. Imitation laces, however, were widely known. Some were variations on the earlier muslin work techniques (see fig. 46). Other imitations began with a net ground onto which motifs were appliquéd or embroidered. This collar is made from machine-made net, which has been embroidered with white thread. USA; mid 19th c.; white cotton net, embroidered with white linen; 3¾" by 12¾"

Embroidered Net and Crochet

With the founding in 1830 of the modern nation of Belgium, the lace-making industries of Europe saw a regeneration. However, intricate hand-made bobbin lace was time-consuming and difficult to produce, and very rarely did American housewives attempt it. In 1830 *Godey's* stated simply, "The making of lace is not now among the pursuits of ladies; it will, therefore, be unnecessary to enter into its details."[14] Instead a number of simple techniques evolved to simulate the delicate hand-made laces from England, France, and Belgium. The most widely known was embroidered or darned net (fig. 48). Embroidered net imitated Brussels point lace. Its popularity was made possible through the availability of machine-made net, which served as a ground fabric for the entire piece.[15]

From 1838 to 1846 crochet emerged as a fashionable form of fancy work.[16] The introduction (or, rather, reintroduction, since crochet was an ancient art) was accompanied by countless pattern books and instructional manuals. Like canvas work, crochet instruction was well suited to the printed word, supplemented by a few illustrations. Once the basic chain stitch and a few variations were explained, the needleworker could follow any number of patterns. Unlike canvas work, crochet patterns needed neither illustrations nor color. A system of

[14] *Godey's Lady's Book* 1 (1830): 233.

[15] This contrasts with hand-made bobbin lace and needle lace, in which the net ground alternates with pattern areas.

[16] Caulfeild and Saward say that crochet became popular in England in 1838, when "patterns were printed and cottons manufactured." (Sophia Frances Anne Caulfeild and Blanche C. Saward, *The Dictionary of Needlework: An Encyclopedia of Artistic, Plain and Fancy Needlework* [London: A. C. Cowan, 1882], 102). Lambert puts the beginning at about 1840. Crochet instructions were included in the anonymous American books published by J. S. Redfield in 1843. *Godey's Lady's Book* introduced the fad to a larger American readership in 1846.

shorthand (not unlike that used today) evolved to tell the needle-woman how to make the most elaborate socks, caps, skirts, and jackets.

Needlework and the Social Structure

In the early nineteenth century, silk embroideries, samplers, and fine muslin work had been the particular privilege of affluent women and their daughters. The materials were expensive, and the skills were learned only through costly lessons. Not so with Berlin work and other mid-century embroideries. The relatively modest cost of the materials and the level of skill required made the techniques available to a much wider segment of the population. As a result, the number and types of patterns and the wide price range catered to the larger consuming public. For a few pennies a woman could buy a small, one-color booklet of patterns suitable for bookmarks or needle cases. For a bit more, she could purchase a hand-painted pattern the size of a slipper or a pair of suspenders. For several dollars, however, she could obtain one of the very large full-color patterns meant for fire screens and framed pictures.[17]

Social change as well as moderate costs helped make decorative needlework available to the middle classes. In the early years of the nineteenth century, a middle-class existence allowed women little spare time. A woman in this social group spent her days doing household chores, helping with her husband's business, and taking care of her children. But after 1830 she was more likely to employ a domestic servant to assist with the chores. Her husband's business was usually farther from home and off-limits to her. And her children now attended school. Clearly she needed a pastime to fill the free hours. What better diversion could she find than to produce lovely embroideries? Needlework was already considered the quintessential ladylike art. And if a middle-class husband had to tolerate wearing an embroidered vest or pair of suspenders, at least he knew that his wife's days were being spent in genteel occupations.

The small size of the projects women undertook at this time served a very practical purpose. A small piece of needlework was completely transportable. A woman could carry a sock on knitting needles in her pocket, or a half-made beaded bag in a small cardboard sewing box. Sewing helped pass the time when visiting with friends, making a long journey, or listening to children recite lessons. This social aspect of embroidery cannot be overemphasized.

Small objects were frequently given as gifts for birthdays or holidays or as mourning tokens. A pair of canvas work slippers could be given to a father, uncle, or brother; a small pincushion or needle case, to a mother, sister, or best friend. Many of these objects contain some hint

[17] Some recent publications have stated that Berlin patterns cost as much as 40 pounds. However, this is a misquotation of Lambert and other early writers, who actually said that the original or prototype pattern could cost that much. Copies made from that pattern, even if hand-colored, were far less costly.

of their having been given as gifts. Some are inscribed simply "Remember me" or "For Papa," while others have small scraps of paper bearing the legend, "Given to me by . . . on the occasion of . . ." The more personalized the gift, the more cherished it became. *Godey's* recommended hairwork gifts, to "insure [sic] that they do actually wear the memento they prize, and not a fabric substitute for it, as we fear has sometimes been the case."[18]

Hair carried great significance. As a gift, human hair made the giver feel that she was sharing a part of herself. And hair outlasted the body. After a person's death, bits of hair became a memento, a keepsake for friends and relatives to cherish. As she lay dying, little Eva, in *Uncle Tom's Cabin,* makes a point of cutting her hair so that she can give a small lock to each of the servants, saying, "I want to give you something that, when you look at it, you shall always remember me."[19]

Needlework and Philanthropy

The idea that women could use their embroidery as a means of raising money for charity developed in the early part of the century. As the country grew, new church congregations formed, each of which needed to construct new buildings. The men contributed money, but the women gave what they had—their time. The money these women raised through the sale of small objects made a difference. The Synod of North Carolina, for example, reported "several examples of female societies which have been active in doing good. One small society, in a town where there was no appropriate house of worship, determined that one should be erected. From the sale of needle work they obtained two hundred dollars, and by other means, they increased the sum until they were able to erect a church which cost twelve hundred dollars."[20]

In England such sales of donated embroidery were called "fancy fairs," a term that was used in this country as well. The early embroidery manuals recognized the popularity of fancy fairs and regularly provided ideas and patterns for new projects. Many of the small decorative objects in mid-Victorian homes can be attributed to the charitable instincts of the women who made them and their friends who purchased them.

In addition to making items for charities to sell, some women formed sewing groups that made clothing and home furnishings for those less fortunate than themselves. One such group was the Dorcas Society, mentioned by Fanny Trollope in her *Domestic Manners of the Americans* (1832), which had several independent chapters throughout the country.[21] The New York Dorcas Society, founded in 1833, was an auxiliary of the Female Assistance Society. Its purpose, according to its constitution, was "to make up articles of Clothing for the Sick Poor of

[18] *Godey's Lady's Book* 41 (1850): 377.

[19] Harriet Beecher Stowe, *Uncle Tom's Cabin* (1852; reprint ed., New York: Dodd, Mead & Co., 1952), 286.

[20] Ladies Magazine, 1, no. 2 (Feb. 1828): 96.

[21] The society was named after Dorcas, who, as the Bible relates, was raised up from the dead because she had spent her life making garments for the poor (Acts 9:36–42). See Fanny Trollope, *Domestic Manners of the Americans* (1832; reprint ed., Oxford and New York: Oxford University Press, 1984), 240–41.

the city, which shall be given to the Parent Society for distribution."[22] The records of the organization show that a core group of women met regularly on Fridays from eleven to two at a Manhattan church.[23]

Needlework as Pastime and Duty

Women sewed because they were taught over and over again that they should not remain idle. "An idle woman is a poor and useless thing," preached one male author. "A *do-nothing* young lady," he continues, "is most assuredly pitied and despised by those whose good opinion she is most anxious to secure."[24] Harriet Beecher Stowe expressed a similar thought in *Uncle Tom's Cabin* by contrasting two heroines. The woman from industrious, Puritan New England carries her crochet with her, while the stereotypical southern belle sits around all day doing nothing. Clearly Stowe, with her New England upbringing, sees the northern woman as a more estimable character.

Throughout the mid-century all woman sewed. It was second nature. Mrs. Farrar could declare quite comfortably in her 1838 etiquette manual, "A woman who does not know how to sew is as deficient in her education as a man who cannot write."[25] Louisa May Alcott made no fewer than 40 references to sewing and sewing tools in *Little Women*. Harriet Beecher Stowe, describing a group of travelers and their respective diversions, summed up the situation: "The boat swept proudly away from the shore, and all went on merrily, as before. Men talked, and loafed, and read, and smoked. Women sewed, and children played, and the boat passed on her way."[26]

[22] *The Fifty Third Annual Report of the New York Female Assistance Society for the Relief and Religious Instruction of the Sick-Poor* (New York: Edward O. Jenkins, 1866).

[23] Ibid.

[24] John Mather Austin, *Golden Steps to Respectability, Usefulness, and Happiness* (Auburn, N.Y.: Derby, Miller and Co., 1850), 95.

[25] Mrs. John Farrar, *The Young Lady's Friend* (Boston: American Stationers' Co., John B. Russell, 1838), 121.

[26] Stowe, *Uncle Tom's Cabin*, 123.

CHAPTER THREE

Civil War
and
Technological
Revolution

1860–1876

I n the history of American needlework, the mid-Victorian years—
1860 to 1876—were an era of transition, a time of both hardship and
prosperity, a bridge between the prim and sedate era of canvas work
and the eclectic era of silk tea cloths. At the beginning of the period
the Civil War divided the nation. At the end, machinery threatened
the existence of hand sewing and embroidery. Wartime drastically
affected the lives and pursuits of American women. It affected the
materials that were available to them, the purposes for which they
made goods, and the design of those goods. Following the war, a new
abundance of materials prompted larger and more elaborate needle-
works. The same era saw the beginning of the British Aesthetic Movement, which sowed the seeds for the new embroideries of the last
quarter of the century.

Needlework and the Civil War

As war approached, the most immediate problem that women could
address was the need for new uniforms. Many of the existing sewing
societies merely shifted their direction and added patriotic fervor to
their weekly sewing meetings. Judith Brockenbrough of Alexandria,
Virginia, wrote, "We must all work for our country. Our soldiers must
be equipped. Our parlor was the rendezvous for our neighborhood, and

our sewing-machine was in requisition for weeks. Scissors and needles were plied by all. The daily scene was most animated. The fires of our enthusiasm and patriotism were burning all the while to a degree which might have been consuming, but that our tongues served as safety-valves. Oh, how we worked and talked, and excited each other!"[1]

The need for military clothing continued throughout the war, although in the areas of heavy fighting, the supply of suitable materials dwindled. There, the emphasis changed from splendor to functionality; making warm winter clothing was far more important than making a handsome uniform or a silk flag. It took increasing skill and ingenuity to make garments from inappropriate materials. The work was rough on the hands, but the women took great pride in their sacrifice and their new-found talents. For women who had grown up in the midst of luxury, the manufacture of a simple straw hat or a knitted undershirt brought a tremendous sense of accomplishment.

Only when the soldiers' clothing was completed could the women attend to their own needs. In this task, again, the women drew on previously unknown abilities. Old clothes were cut apart and remade, then patched over and over again. Some women started wearing homespun in order to save their calico gowns. Shoes became scarce ("I have had such a search for shoes this week and am disgusted with shopping," wrote Sarah Morgan in 1862),[2] so women knitted or crocheted slippers. But the greatest problem was obtaining a good-looking and well-trimmed bonnet. One woman wrote wistfully, "I could make lovely flowers if I had materials."[3] The image of Scarlet O'Hara making a dress out of a pair of curtains is not at all far-fetched.

For the population that lived outside the areas of conflict, the hardship was not as great, but the effect of the war was the same. As far north as Boston, women formed societies that made military clothing for the soldiers. Fancy fairs, once held to raise money for charities, were now held to support the war effort. The fairs offered for sale a wide variety of new and second-hand merchandise such as lithographs, dry goods, photographs, and houseplants. Women's work played a small but important part. At the Great Central Fair held in Philadelphia in 1864, for example, the bookmarkers, Berlin work, and beadwork on sale had been made and contributed not only by the wealthy, but also by "poor needle-women, who have found spare moments to throw in their mite to the succor of our Soldier Brothers."[4] Although the fairs created a more festive mood than was known in the areas closer to the fighting, the need to raise money was still felt urgently.

A glance at *Godey's Lady's Book* for six months after the war commenced shows how little the conflict affected the fashionable scene in the northern cities. There were only two references to war: a sentimental tale about a girl who loved her twin brother so much that she cut

[1] [Judith Brockenbrough McGuire], *Diary of a Southern Refugee During the War* (New York: Hale and Sons, 1867), excerpted in Katherine M. Jones, *Heroines of Dixie: Confederate Women Tell Their Story of the War* (Indianapolis: Bobbs-Merrill, 1955), 32.

[2] Sarah Morgan Dawson, *A Confederate Girl's Diary*, ed. Warrington Dawson (Boston: Houghton Mifflin, 1913), excerpted in Jones, *Heroines of Dixie*, 133.

[3] Mrs. Roger A. Pryor, *Reminiscences of Peace and War* (New York: Macmillan, 1904), excerpted in Jones, *Heroines of Dixie*, 202.

[4] *Philadelphia Great Central Fair for the U.S.: Philadelphia Sanitary Fair Catalogue & Guide* (N.P.: 1864), 19.

49

Although almost all Berlin patterns were produced in Germany, many printers catered to the foreign market. This portrait of Abraham Lincoln was produced by Louis Gluer, a well-known publisher from Berlin, whose works have been dated from 1846 to 1868. During and after the Civil War, Lincoln achieved the same mythic proportions as George Washington, and his image was reproduced on countless decorative art forms.

Berlin, Germany; ca. 1860–1870; paper, printed and painted; 17″ by 15½″

her hair and replaced him in battle, and a series of notices for books on how to become a good soldier. The military braiding used on women's and children's clothing reflected the reaction of European arbiters of fashion to the Crimean War and other European conflicts—not the reaction of American ladies to their own war. There were hints that certain materials had become hard to find, but war was not mentioned as the cause of the scarcity. Only a few obviously patriotic symbols, such as portraits of Abraham Lincoln, were adopted by northern needleworkers (fig. 49).

Following the Civil War American needlework underwent significant changes, many of which can be related to improvements in technology. A long period of inventions in the field of sewing, embroidering, and lacemaking finally resulted in viable machinery and the growth of garment factories. Chemical discoveries led to new synthetic dyes, which provided the needleworker with a new color palette. Changes in retail marketing and mailing brought goods to a wider public. And an abundance of materials led to superfluities of design.

Sewing Machines

The invention that had the greatest impact on plain sewing at this time was the sewing machine. Many inventors worked simultaneously during the first half of the nineteenth century to produce a workable sewing machine. Although some were in use as early as the 1840s, their availability to a significant percentage of the population can be traced to the late 1850s. Their impact on plain sewing (i.e., hand sewing), therefore, must date to the beginning of the 1860s. *McElroy's Philadelphia Directory* for 1855, for example, lists only two sewing machine salesmen; in 1860, nineteen were listed. Only a few more years would pass before sewing machines were available for purchase even in rural areas.

By the end of this era, nearly every woman in the United States owned or had access to a sewing machine. Not only the appearance of sewing changed, but the actual task as well. Sewing by machine is a far less sociable occupation than sewing by hand. In earlier decades women would congregate in the formal drawing room and sew as a group. Now, even though table-top models were available, the work had become far less portable. Rarely would more than one machine be found in a private home. As a result, sewing became a solitary, not a group, occupation. The new machines were usually placed in the room where the family gathered, and a woman sewed in the midst of her family. But it was not as easy for her to communicate with others while she operated her machine, since she had to focus on her work more carefully. No longer would etiquette manuals suggest all sorts of tasks (like listening to children's lessons) that could be done while sewing.

Just as sewing machines were becoming an essential piece of furniture in the Victorian parlor, they were also revolutionizing professional garment manufacture. Women who sewed for a living could not afford a machine and increasingly found themselves working in factories for an entrepreneur with the capital to purchase a large number of them. This took professional stitchers out of the home and disrupted family life. In the shoe industry in Lynn, Massachusetts, for example, women had accomplished the binding of uppers while taking care of their children. By the mid-century, working-class women were confined in unpleasant factories for much of their day. At the same time, the development of

50

This typically massive mid-Victorian pattern combines naturalistic motifs with the new interest in medieval themes. Note the predominant peacock, the large flowers, and the castle in the background. Such hand-painted designs were works of art in their own right and were occasionally displayed in homes as finished pieces. This example was elaborately framed and hung on the walls of a home in Bucks County, Pennsylvania.
Germany; ca. 1860–1870; paper, printed and painted; 28½″ by 23½″

51

A perfect example of mid-Victorian super-fluities can be found in the large hairwork pieces of the 1860s. Compare this work with the much more subtle use of hair in fig. 41. Works of this scale were generally made in professional shops, several of which advertised in the directories of major cities. According to written documentation, how-ever, this work was made by Anna Hicks Deagle (1845–1931) when she was 23 years old.

Northern New England; 1868; hair, wire, glass beads, wax, silk; 27¼″ by 21¼″

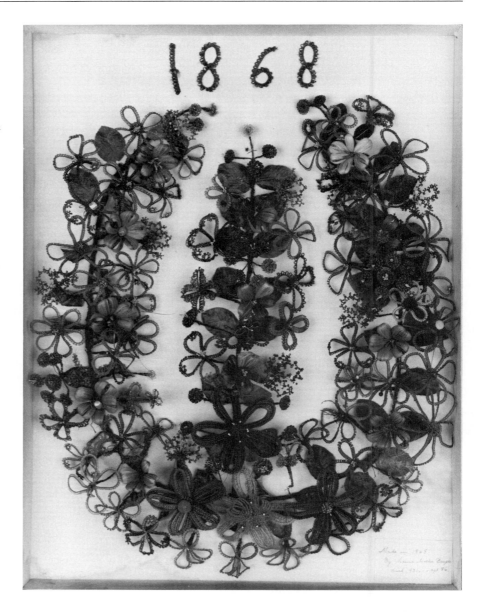

garment factories meant a larger supply of ready-made clothing and a decreased need for women to provide the garments and home furnishings for their families.

With the beginning of factories, sewing became an occupation, rather than a household chore, a craft, or a refined pastime. Girls were still urged to acquire the skill, but only so that they might have an occupation to fall back on, should they find themselves destitute. By the end of the era, it was no longer as fashionable to sit around in groups sewing and talking. The Dorcas societies still met, but annual reports reveal that the members gathered to cut rather than to sew garments. The unsewn pieces were given to needy people to stitch together for themselves.

52
*This unusual wreath is made from plush
balls and thread-covered coiled wire. The
pen and ink drawing on paper placed in the
center of the wreath reflects the importance
of home and family life, for under the word
"home" is depicted a family of birds in a
nest.*
Farmington, Maine; ca. 1870; covered
wire and red, green, pink, yellow, and
white wool, attached to paper and off-
white silk ground; 38" by 35½"

Embroidery Machines

Plain sewing was not the only branch of needlework to be affected by the machine age; embroidery was also vulnerable. The first embroidery machines, which were available in the 1830s, used a double-pointed needle, held by pincers and pushed through the fabric to a second set of pincers below. The single-thread embroidery closely resembled that produced by hand. Although the machines could handle 180 needles at once, those needles still had to be hand-threaded, and the size of the motif was limited by the length of thread available. These early machines, which were few and far between, were used primarily to manufacture embroidered ribbons. Since embroidered ribbons were a new fashion, no embroiderers, either professional or amateur, were immediately put out of work.

During the 1860s this technology was combined with the two-thread sewing machine. By 1867 the new "Schiffli" embroidery machine was turning heads at the Paris World Exhibition, and by 1875 models had been imported and used by the New York firm of Kursheedt's. Once these embroidery machines dominated the market, embroidery was no longer even an occupation; it was a factory job. Even though a considerable amount of hand embroidery continued to be produced, much of it was done by professionals. Therefore, the interest of home sewers in embroidering their own clothing and household linens decreased dramatically during this era.

Postwar Needlework

Despite the competition of factory-made needlework, women continued to produce embroideries in the home. The new work differed from that of the prewar era not in style or technique, but in the quantity and scale of projects. American women embroidered less, but the size of individual works increased. For example, their canvas work pieces were extremely elaborate, using a palette inspired by the new synthetic dyes (fig. 50). Instead of subtly embroidered white bed coverings, they preferred patchwork quilts made from brightly colored silks. Rather than small pieces of hairwork jewelry, they made elaborate wired hairwork wreaths (figs. 51, 52).

Four factors are responsible for the exaggerated designs of mid-Victorian needlework. First, Americans were influenced by English and French fashions, which saw the same growth. Second, larger works and wilder patterns can be viewed as part of a psychological reaction to the end of the Civil War. Third, the machine age had brought a wealth of new and inexpensive materials; American factories produced new cot-

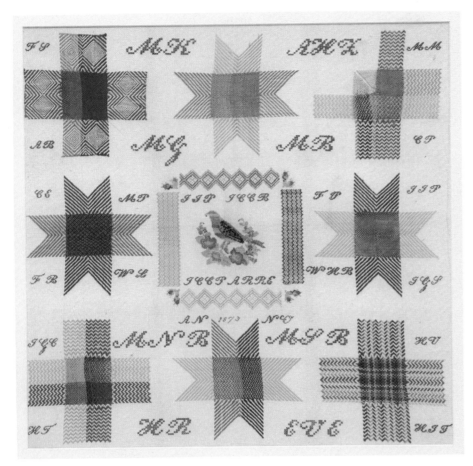

53
In a darning sampler, the embroiderer cut small square holes in a piece of linen, and then filled the holes with colored thread. The darning threads formed a variety of patterned weaves, such as twill, herringbone, and damask. Darning samplers are more often datable to the late eighteenth or early nineteenth century than to the late nineteenth. This example, which is dated 1873, shows beautiful technique. It also shows the new patterns, colors, and threads available to the mid-century needlewoman. Kinderhook, N.Y.; 1873; white linen, embroidered with multicolored cotton; 17³⁄₄″ by 17¹⁄₄″

ton embroidery threads, patterns, silk fabrics, and more (fig. 53). Fourth, with the factory system came a new entrepreneurial class, a *nouveau riche* group who had cash to spend, yet had not been schooled in the accepted tastes of the world of old money.

A perfect example of the growth in the scale of needlework projects can be found in perforated card work. When the technique of embroidering on a piece of cardboard was first introduced, projects were minute (as small as a few inches square). By 1860 the largest perforated card projects measured approximately 9 inches by 12 inches. But in the mid-1870s, Americans took a liking to large mottoes, which were often

54

After the Civil War, large punched paper mottoes were a popular needlework form. In addition to hanging on parlor and dining room walls, mottoes were framed and hung above interior doors. Among the first mottoes used was the well-known "Home Sweet Home." Unlike many perforated cards that bear this inscription, the present example is remarkable for both the use of color and the variety of stitches.
Northern New England; ca. 1870; printed punched paper, embroidered with multicolored wool; 15" by 19"

embroidered in thick wool on a heavy punched cardboard (figs. 54, 55). Mottoes were usually placed either above the door frame or along the wall of less formal rooms. Biblical quotations and sentimental sayings predominated, the most popular being "Home Sweet Home." The sayings probably evolved from those used for bookmarks. *Peterson's Magazine* presented patterns of sayings identified as suitable for both bookmarks and mottoes. Less well known were pictorial patterns and political images, such as portraits of Lincoln or Washington.

Mottoes were popular because they were new and innovative and because they were inexpensive and easy to make. Patterns could be hand drawn on perforated cards, but preprinted boards with fairly large and widely spaced holes were more often used. Unlike Berlin patterns, preprinted cards were manufactured by several American firms. Advertisements for the printed cards indicate that they could be purchased for as little as a penny. The embroiderer finished the work merely by covering the design with wool or silk threads. Many stitches were possible, but a simple diagonal stitch was the favorite. The finished work was often laid over gilt paper (which would show through the holes of the uncovered background) and enclosed in a simple, home-made frame.

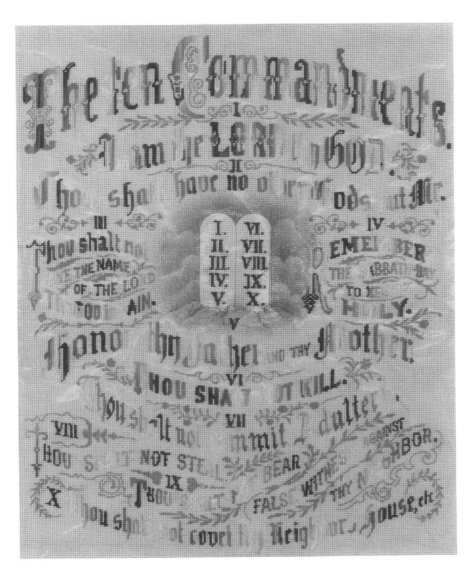

55
Like small bookmarks, wall mottoes frequently employed biblical sayings and phrases. The embroiderer of this large picture of the ten commandments purchased a preprinted perforated board. The motto is worked entirely in tent stitch, but surface interest is achieved through the use of variegated yarn, dyed progressive shades of yellow, orange, and brown. As was customary, the entire work is backed with silver paper, which appears through the unfilled holes. New Hampshire; ca. 1870–1880; printed punched paper, embroidered with multicolored wool; 19¼" by 15¼"

Publications

America's new self-sufficiency produced another development in the world of needlework. Although many English books were still available in this country, American publishers lagged behind their European competitors. Only a few new needlework books were published in America between 1860 and 1876. Earlier books were regularly reprinted, as were collections of magazine articles, but these all reiterated the same pre-1860 material. Even the new books are largely redundant, with virtually the same patterns and instructions for canvas work, white embroidery, knitting, and crochet. In contrast, books like *Beeton's Book of Needlework,* published in England in 1870, contain instructions and patterns for tatting, appliqué, and point lace, three techniques that would become popular in the United States several years later.

The exception was *Harper's Bazar,* which began publication in 1867. The new magazine gave patterns and instructions for a wide selection of ambitious needlework projects. Far more up-to-date than *Peterson's* and *Godey's, Harper's* introduced the latest needlework fads from Britain. It was the only American publication of the era to include design ideas from the new Aesthetic Movement, which had been developing in Britain since the Crystal Palace Exhibition in 1851. Never identified as English, and presented without fanfare, the new patterns in *Harper's* did not gain too much attention. In the mid-1870s the magazine decreased the number and scope of needlework projects, an editorial move that suggests that readers were not responding to the new ideas.

Meanwhile, England was experiencing a great reform in decorative design. An understanding of American needlework in the last decade of the nineteenth century requires at least a brief look at the English mid-century reform movement.

Eastlake and Morris

In England, Berlin work and other mid-century needlework styles had begun to lose favor as early as 1850. British designers fought against what they considered the gushing sentimentality, superfluities, and unoriginality of the counted-stitch canvas works, hair works, and the like. Charles Eastlake, a leading British furniture designer, was particularly vocal on the subject. He referred to the overdesigned mid-Victorian interiors using words like "absurd," "ridiculous," and "vulgar," and he breathed a sigh of relief when he finally saw ladies "relinquishing the ridiculous custom of endeavoring to reproduce, in cross-stitch worsted-work, the pictures of Landseer and Frank Stone."[5]

[5] Charles L. Eastlake, *Hints on Household Taste in Furniture, Upholstery, and Other Details* (Boston: James R. Osgood and Co., 1877), 12.

Although Eastlake and other experts on home decoration spoke against Berlin wool work, they offered few alternatives for the embroiderer. William Morris, on the other hand, presented tangible new designs and techniques. More famous for his printed and woven textiles, Morris had a significant influence on the world of embroidery. He began experimenting with needlework in the late 1850s, with designs based on historic textiles such as figured Renaissance tapestries and Persian carpets. Later works were primarily floral. His depiction of figures and flowers was less realistic than that found in Berlin wool work. Morris felt that a completely naturalistic rendering was "cheap and commonplace," and he advised against overuse of shading. He rejected the counted stitches, preferring the freer satin stitch with a loosely twisted crewel yarn. He even rejected the standard palette, developing his own dyes.

Morris was an artist, yet he was also a manufacturer. He had no intention of encouraging domestic embroidery; his goal was to improve the quality of mass-produced arts. His company produced designs by commission, with emphasis on large hangings, curtains, and folding screens. The finished products often sold for £100 or more, making them a luxury item. Although a woman could order a design and work it herself, the projects were so vast that even some begun by Morris's wife remain unfinished to this day. Morris designs were not available in the United States, since he refused to export his work. Wealthy American travelers brought some items home, but Morris embroideries hung primarily in the houses of a small, elite group of wealthy Britons.

The Royal School of Art Needlework

Morris's embroidery designs might have remained relatively unknown had it not been for the Royal School of Art Needlework. The school was founded in 1872 to train and employ working-class women in the craft of needlework. By supporting the school, wealthy women satisfied their social obligations to charity and secured a supply of well-designed home furnishings. Begun by a wealthy Englishwoman, the school received the patronage of Queen Victoria and several of her children. Lady Marian Alford, the well-known needlework author, served as vice-president. In addition to using William Morris designs, the school boasted the talents of Walter Crane and Sir Edward Coley Burne-Jones, whose names were almost as well known as Morris's. It established a number of affiliated groups and even published an instructional manual.

The Royal School of Art Needlework made designs available to the general public in two ways. The school operated like a factory, employing needlewomen to embroider objects for special commissions or for sale in the school's outlets. In addition, the school sold cloth with the designs drawn or partially worked for ambitious domestic embroiderers. Many diverse objects were available. The large hangings and screens were the most impressive and the most costly. We suspect that the largest trade was in the small table mats, doilies, and tidies (pads put on chair backs to protect the upholstery from hair oil) that decorated mid- and late Victorian homes.

The Royal School worked diligently to gain a national and international reputation, and it was only a matter of time before its influence would reach America. That time would come during the Centennial Exhibition of 1876.

CHAPTER FOUR

*The
Aesthetic
Movement
in America*

1876–1900

In 1876 the United States celebrated its centennial by holding a massive international exhibition in Philadelphia. The mood of the exhibition was optimistic; the United States entered its second century with every intention of becoming a major manufacturing nation. Displays in the industrial pavilions celebrated the remarkable technological accomplishments of the previous decades. At the same time, a revolution of sorts was in evidence in the Women's Pavilion, which featured large displays of foreign and domestic needlework. Competing for attention were the usual large canvas work pictures and the new embroideries produced by the Royal School of Art Needlework in London. According to contemporary critics, the British embroideries stole the show, launching a new craze among America's needleworkers.

The contrast between the old and the new works was remarkable. The canvas work embroideries exhibited in Philadelphia were such typical pieces as "portraits worked in silk or embroidered in worsted . . . of Queen Victoria, Mr. Gladstone, Prince Albert. . . . An elaborate picture in worsted work represented the 'Death of George Douglas at the Battle of Langside' . . . and [there was] a picture in needlework of Abraham and Hagar."[1] However, across the hall was a "magnificent tent, or booth, constructed of purple velvet hangings, and ornamented with a superb collection of specimens of embroidery and needlework. An exquisitely worked scroll over the entrance told us that this was the

[1] James D. McCabe, *The Illustrated History of the Centennial Exhibition* (Philadelphia: National Publishing Co., 1876), 658.

pavilion of the 'Royal School of Art and Needlework [*sic*].' "[2] The magnificent hanging, specially made for the exhibition, was intended to make a splash, and it did. The critics and the public were impressed. Almost immediately American women abandoned their counted-stitch Berlin work to follow the new fad, called "art needlework" or "Kensington work."

Candace Wheeler and the Society of Decorative Art

One visitor to Philadelphia was Mrs. Candace Wheeler, who is often credited with the spread of art needlework in the United States. Although she did not accomplish this single-handedly, she was certainly very influential. Candace Wheeler possessed the two attributes held by the founders of the Royal School: she wanted to be charitable, and she wanted to improve the quality of needlework. The first intention derived from her position in society and her wealth. The second was based on her personal qualifications and background. In her earlier years she had studied painting abroad, and in this country had more than a passing acquaintance with such artists as George Inness, Albert Bierstadt, and William Merritt Chase.

Unlike those visitors who were merely impressed by the splendor of the display, Mrs. Wheeler saw the practical possibilities of the Royal School and the needlework it promoted. Recalling not the elaborate draperies but the embroidered tidies, she stated: "The actual specimens of the Kensington work were to my mind very simple and almost inadequate. . . . It seemed to me a very simple sort of effort to have gained the vogue of a new art, and I saw that it was easily within the compass of almost every woman. It required far less ability than painting china or more or less ambitious pictures, or making elaborate needle-books for sale among one's friends."[3]

In response to the exhibition, Mrs. Wheeler persuaded her society friends to organize the Society of Decorative Art in New York. Like the Royal School, the Society of Decorative Art aimed "to give a practical direction to the art talent of the women of the country."[4] The society encouraged several branches of decorative arts, but needlework was always the most important component. To accomplish its goal, the new institution held classes, maintained a lending library, and published a biweekly journal called the *Art Interchange*. A shop was opened to accept needlework for sale on a consignment basis.

The Society of Decorative Art was never as successful as its British predecessor at improving public taste. Although it followed the principles of the Royal School, it made a few important and unfortunate changes in its practice. Like the English institution, it taught technique, not design, so that the embroiderers graduated with no idea of

[2] Ibid., 387. A photograph of the hanging appears in Doreen Bolger Burke et al. *In Pursuit of Beauty: Americans and the Aesthetic Movement* (New York: Metropolitan Museum of Art/Rizzoli, 1986), 97.

[3] Candace Wheeler, *Yesterdays in a Busy Life* (New York and London: Harper & Brothers, 1918), 212.

[4] *Art Interchange* 1, no. 1 (18, Sept. 1878): 1.

56
The term "art needlework" was coined to refer to embroidered pictures that, unlike Berlin work, employed free-hand stitches and emulated painting. Of great importance in American art needlework were shading techniques. Note the three-dimensional quality given to both the basket and the red cherries in this picture.
USA; ca. 1890; white linen, embroidered with red, white, light brown, green, and yellow silk; 19½" by 22½"

what constituted a well-designed work. Lack of design training was not a problem in England, because the embroiderers were always supplied with high-quality designs to follow. The first members of the American society used both the designs and the techniques of the English, but soon found these too restricting. Said the independent Americans, "The English system is not slavishly followed; what is best in the method is adopted, and liberty given for individual taste, from which is resulting a distinctive American style, which even now bears favorable comparison with that of older schools."[5] This allowance for individual taste led to designs of very poor quality, and the Committee of Admissions, which judged all works brought to the sales shops, had to turn many away.

Finally, the committee established weekly meetings where members brought original designs to be critiqued. Far from solving the problem, this step permitted American embroidery design to be dictated by a committee of virtually untrained socialites. It is not surprising that Mrs. Wheeler and Louis C. Tiffany, the only two artists on the committee, resigned after two years. Stating that "philanthropy and art are not natural sisters,"[6] Wheeler next became involved in two separate institutions. One, the Woman's Exchange, was purely charitable in nature and sold all goods donated to it regardless of quality. The other, Associated Artists, was a for-profit cooperative of professional designers.

[5] Ibid.

[6] Wheeler, *Yesterdays*, 223.

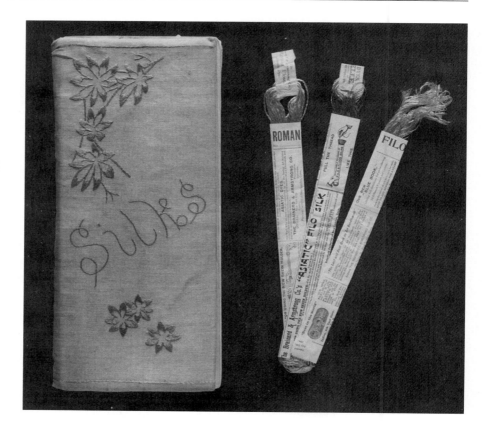

57
The owner of this hand-made book used it to keep her embroidery silk in order. The assorted skeins contained in the book were manufactured by M. Heminway & Sons and by the Brainerd & Armstrong Company. The brilliant colors are all guaranteed to be permanent, though the purchaser is advised to use Ivory soap or "other pure soap" for washing. The threads were patented in 1894 and 1895, when the silk embroidery craft was just becoming popular. USA; 1895–1900; book of paper and cardboard, covered with light blue linen embroidered with red silk thread; 10⅞" by 4¾"

[7] Candace Wheeler, *The Development of Embroidery in America* (New York and London: Harper & Brothers, 1921), 108–114.

In the latter institution she would influence mostly the needlework made by trained embroiderers for very wealthy customers. However, she continued to observe and write about all trends in American needlework.

Mrs. Wheeler was conscious of national expression in the field of needlework design. She knew the work of Morris and the other English embroiderers, and she could identify how American works differed in subject matter, style of depiction, color, and materials. The Americans used just as many flowers as their British counterparts, but they also had a passion for pictorial scenes. They rejected the vision of Morris and his contemporaries and their emphasis on two-dimensional interpretations. Americans loved shading and any other technique that made the embroidery more realistic (fig. 56). Color was a major point of difference, for the Americans did not much care for the subtleties of shade that Morris had gone out of his way to develop, and their works were much bolder in coloration. Finally, the Americans soon grew tired of wool, and as soon as American silk yarns were available, they adopted the shinier material without hesitation (fig. 57).[7]

The Society of Decorative Art trained and employed only a few hundred women at any one time, so its direct influence was somewhat limited. However, Mrs. Wheeler's vision included a national network of affiliated societies. As many as 30 were established across the country. The most important were located in major cities like Boston, Chicago, and Philadelphia, where the societies benefited from the support and the facilities of major art museums. Similar societies were accessible to the residents of smaller cities, such as St. Louis, Charleston, Ithaca, and Saratoga. Though autonomous, these institutions looked to the parent organization for inspiration. And although the original purpose of the society was to train working-class women, the fad for the new needlework spread upward to middle-class domestic embroiderers.

Publications

As important as the Society of Decorative Arts was to the development of art needlework in America, it is unlikely that the new ideas would have spread so far in so brief a time had publishers and manufacturers not realized the potential profit involved. American publications of this era included women's magazines, needlework journals, and book series (fig. 58). Unlike the craft societies discussed above, the producers of the new needlework literature were more interested in revenue than in promoting good designs. But this flood of publications was powerful enough to alter the style of American needlework.

Godey's Lady's Book and Peterson's Magazine continued to serve their well-established and fairly wealthy readership. To these publications were added in the 1880s the Ladies Home Journal and the Home-Maker, which aimed at a less affluent, more rural audience. Both magazines regularly mentioned the Royal School of Art Needlework and included designs that had originated in the school, but the quality of the patterns was poor. Mrs. Wheeler excoriated these publications—the "wretched fashion journals that have flooded the country with discordant designs, made by cheap designers, regardless of or in ignorance of the laws of color and of composition."[8] The readership figures and letters to the editor, however, indicate that these forms of the fashionable ideals were very popular.

Hardbound volumes containing patterns and instructions were still mostly English in origin. The most readily available in this country were those by Countess Alford, Samuel Orchard Beeton, and Caulfeild and Saward. Many American books relied on the British manuals for information, and were produced by publishers who presented large series of books on unrelated topics. Lucretia Peabody Hale, better known as the author of the Peterkin Papers, edited a series produced by S. W. Tilton in Boston. Each of her books contains some notice such as "reprinted with additions from the English" or "compiled from valuable sources." The most original American work of the era was The Ladies' Guide to Needlework by S. Annie Frost,[9] although even this

[8] Art Amateur 18, no. 2 (Jan. 1888): 46.

[9] S. Annie Frost, The Ladies' Guide to Needlework, Embroidery, etc., Being a Complete Guide to All Kinds of Ladies' Fancy Work, with Full Descriptions of All the Various Stitches and Materials, and a Large Number of Illustrations for Each Variety of Work (New York: Adam & Bishop, 1877; reprint ed., Lopez Island, Wash.: R. L. Shep, 1986).

58

A profusion of printed matter for needle-workers followed close on the heels of the Philadelphia Centennial. Most of the American publications were produced by manufacturers of patterns, thread, and cloth and were given free or sold at minimal cost as promotional tools.

book, on close inspection, looks suspiciously like many of the English works of the period.

Most easily obtainable, however, were a large number of manuals and periodicals produced by manufacturers. The first to appear were issued by patternmakers, such as the Butterick Publishing Company, T. E. Parker, and the Patten Publishing Co. These were followed by publications of the thread and yarn manufacturers, particularly Brainerd & Armstrong, the Dorcas Company, M. Heminway & Sons Silk Co., and the Nonotuck Silk Co. There is no doubt that these firms were motivated by profit. Many of them issued free instructional manuals as premiums for buying their products. All of them wrote directions that called for their own materials. *Dorcas: A Magazine of Woman's Handi-*

work, was named without hesitation for the thread company it endorsed. "It will be noticed," said Laura B. Starr, editor, in the second issue, "that throughout the Magazine we recommend but the one brand of silks and wools. This is because we have tried them and found them most satisfactory, and because all our patterns are made from them, and we know exactly how they will work."[10] Another manufacturer warned: "A lady who places any value at all upon her time, cannot afford to use any silk but *the best.*"[11]

Other magazines and books directly promoted the ideas of the Royal School and the Society of Decorative Art. If these were less mercenary, they offered no better designs. The society's official magazine, the *Art Interchange,* offered patterns and instructions for only the most popular forms of art needlework. Constance Cary Harrison's *Woman's Handiwork in Modern Homes* included a history of the society in addition to many poorly drawn patterns. Louis Higgin, who wrote the Royal School's *Handbook of Embroidery* in 1880, concentrated on technique rather than design. The few patterns included in the *Handbook* are attributed to Morris and others, but they are of poor quality. And although he encouraged needlewomen to be artistic, Higgin only urged readers to draw the pattern on the cloth free-hand rather than trace it. He never encouraged them to try their own designs.

The only publication that offered fine-quality designs during this era was the *Art Amateur,* which was offered for sale by Charles E. Bentley, a pattern publisher in New York. The designs printed in early issues of this publication were also based on those of the Royal School, and are of better quality than those offered in the *Art Interchange.* The articles on needlework are informative and provocative. Many present historic textiles, with very accurate illustrations of actual works of art. Others discuss the difference between "conventional" and realistic renderings. The magazine adopted the ideas of the Aesthetic Movement, declaring: "Love of show for its own sake is vulgar."[12] Like the *Art Interchange,* the *Art Amateur* catered to an elite audience, and its readership, which peaked at 10,000 subscribers, resided primarily in and around New York City.

Patterns

No book or institution encouraged embroiderers to create new and original designs. Many openly discouraged originality. For example, an article in *Dorcas,* entitled "How to Follow Directions," advised readers against trying to make changes in patterns.[13] The patterns referred to were offered for sale by a small number of companies. The most popular were C. E. Bentley, J. F. Ingalls, T. E. Parker, and the Patten Publishing Co. Fancy goods shops sold individual patterns to their customers,

[10] *Dorcas* 1, no. 2 (Feb. 1884): 1.

[11] The Brainerd & Armstrong Co., *Embroidery Lessons, with Colored Studies* (New London, Conn.: Brainerd & Armstrong Co., 1899), 106.

[12] *Art Amateur* 2, no. 3 (Feb. 1880): 60.

[13] *Dorcas* 1, no. 11 (Nov. 1884).

59

Art needlework was commonly used to decorate a wide range of circular tea cloths. The most popular designs employed a variety of realistic flowers and fruits. This design was probably purchased as a punched pattern. The embroiderer was given only the outline of the motifs, not the shading. The work is enriched by a wide hand-made lace border. Tea cloths like this were sold in the consignment shops of the Society of Decorative Art and similar organizations.

Detail; New York or New Jersey; ca. 1890–1900; white linen, embroidered with red, yellow, gold, green, and white silk; 39″ in diameter

or would stamp patterns on fabric brought in by customers. In addition, some stores sold linens that were already stamped and ready to embroider, as well as "commenced goods," that is, partially embroidered linen. Pattern companies promoted sales by offering large sets of designs at reduced rates and by arranging with magazine publishers to offer patterns as incentives to new subscribers.

There were three types of patterns: punched, tissue paper, and heat transfer. The most popular type was made by punching a series of very tiny holes into blank white paper. The pattern was placed directly on the fabric to be embroidered, and a blue powder was sprinkled on top and pounced (i.e., pounded or tapped) down. Then the fabric was pressed with a hot iron to set the powder. Tissue paper patterns were like those available today. They required the embroiderer to trace the design onto the ground fabric with a pencil or a tracing wheel. Transfer patterns, patented by the British firm Briggs and Co., could be applied directly to the fabric with a hot iron.

Silk Embroidery

American expression, as defined by Mrs. Wheeler, was most frequently manifested in embroidered fruit and flowers rendered in the so-called Kensington stitch. By the end of the century, these motifs were particularly used to adorn the array of white linen cloths that covered ladies' tea tables (figs. 59, 60). Describing these in *House Beautiful*, Mrs. Wheeler wrote, "Today is unquestionably an era [which] will go down in the history of the arts as the 'tea-cloth period.' The tea-cloths, where roses drop their embroidered leaves upon white linen, and pale clematis flowers are tangled with cobwebs, or the blossoms of the Indian palm play with lace-winged dragon-flies, are purely American in character."[14]

She was candid in her assessment of the designs for tea cloths. The "application is so naïve and direct that it never occurs to one to bring it before the tribunal of design. In fact, many of these lovely things owe nothing to the art of design; they are simply a laying of flowers upon the altar of the household."[15] But while she did not hold the *design* of the cloths in high esteem, she praised the work of the embroiderer: "We find a great deal of perhaps unconscious knowledge of the rules of art in our modern embroidery upon linen. The color is restrained and delicate, there is no harsh contrast of tone between the whiteness of the linen and the glow of the flowers."[16]

The stitches used in silk needlework were many, but only those based on the satin stitch were regularly used. Two stitches in particular are worth noting. The outline stitch, as its name implies, was formed with a series of back stitches so closely spaced as to make a single

[14] Candace Wheeler, "The Art of Stitchery," *House Beautiful* 5, no. 5 (Apr. 1899): 196.

[15] Ibid.

[16] Ibid.

60

The embroiderer of this piece bought a piece of linen that had the design already stamped on (the blue lines are still visible at the edge of each embroidered area), so she did not have to make any composition decisions. However, the skill, the use of color and shading, and the variety of stitches suggest that the maker of this tea cloth was an accomplished needlewoman. Another indication of the needleworker's skill is the band of drawn work that connects the flower motifs. Detail; New England; ca. 1890–1900; white linen, embroidered with pink, yellow, green, brown, white, and orange silk; 31" in diameter

heavy line. The Kensington stitch, named for the location of the Royal School, was an overlapping satin stitch particularly useful for covering large areas. "With the outline stitches and the Kensington stitches thoroughly mastered," wrote an American author, "an almost unlimited amount and variety of decorative needlework is within your reach. In fact, the greater amount of embroidery shown at the rooms of Decorative Art Societies in this country and England is wrought with the above mentioned stitches alone."[17]

[17] Adelaide E. Heron, *Dainty Work for Pleasure and Profit* (Chicago: Danks & Co., 1891), 31.

Outline Work

The outline stitch prompted a whole new style of art embroidery. Outline work, which was first seen in this country around 1880, resembles a line drawing (fig. 61). There is some relationship between outline work and the tambour work and cord work of earlier decades,[18] although the origin of outline work cannot be explained completely in this way. There is also a stylistic link to the so-called *point Russe* embroidery featured in *Harper's Bazar* in the 1860s.[19] In fact, outline work probably began as a result of the Royal School's and the Decorative Art Society's practice of selling "commenced goods,"[20] which, if left unfinished, would resemble outline work.

Outline work was praised for its artistic quality and for the speed with which it could be produced. One American author wrote, "As the chief beauty of outline work depends upon grace and fidelity to form, it is naturally a craft demanding poetic instinct as well as delicate manipulation. In nothing else wrought with a needle does the worker achieve results so delightfully prompt."[21]

Respectable designers found some merit in the form. Walter Crane, a colleague of William Morris, wrote: "When the design and expression is of a very abstract character, and its decorative effect mainly depends upon the arrangement and quality of line, one would say the simpler the better, since the ideas are conveyed by means of suggestion rather than by any attempt at realization of form in its full substance and colour."[22] Even the high-quality *Art Amateur* gave in and included outline work patterns, though it felt compelled to apologize to its more discriminating readers. In 1880, it prefaced an article on outline work with a somewhat disdainful note: "Most of our city lady readers are already familiar with this kind of work. These designs are not for them, but are given in compliance of requests for information on the subject . . . from ladies at a distance."[23]

Outline work's popularity can be explained by the simplicity of the technique. In many of the wall hangings by Morris and his contemporaries, the entire ground was covered with a variety of satin stitches. In the American version of silk embroidery, the satin stitches filled the pattern areas. In outline work, however, the satin stitches were dispensed with altogether, and only the lines of the pattern were covered with a single or double row of back stitches, called variously "stem" or "outline." Because of its simplicity, outline work was considered appropriate for women "who have neither time, eyesight nor means to indulge in intricate and elaborate needlework."[24]

The pictures of Kate Greenaway, the British book illustrator, were by far the most popular designs for outline work (fig. 62). Greenaway was a true Aesthetic and depicted in line drawings and watercolors "a

[18] *Dorcas*, for example, calls outline embroidery "an adaptation of Indian and Oriental quilting," perhaps referring to tambour work.

[19] *Harper's Bazar* 1 (21 Mar. 1868): 324, and subsequent issues.

[20] Pattern companies, such as Bentley Bros., also sold commenced work. See *Harper's Bazar* 12 (18 Jan. 1879): 50.

[21] Constance Cary Harrison, *Woman's Handiwork in Modern Homes, with Numerous Illustrations and Five Colored Plates from Designs by Samuel Colman, Rosina Emmet, George Gibson, and Others* (New York: Charles Scribner's Sons, 1881).

[22] Walter Crane, "Needlework as a Mode of Artistic Expression," *Magazine of Art* (Jan. 1898): 147–148.

[23] *Art Amateur* 3, no. 5 (Oct. 1880): 102.

[24] Heron, *Dainty Work*, 85.

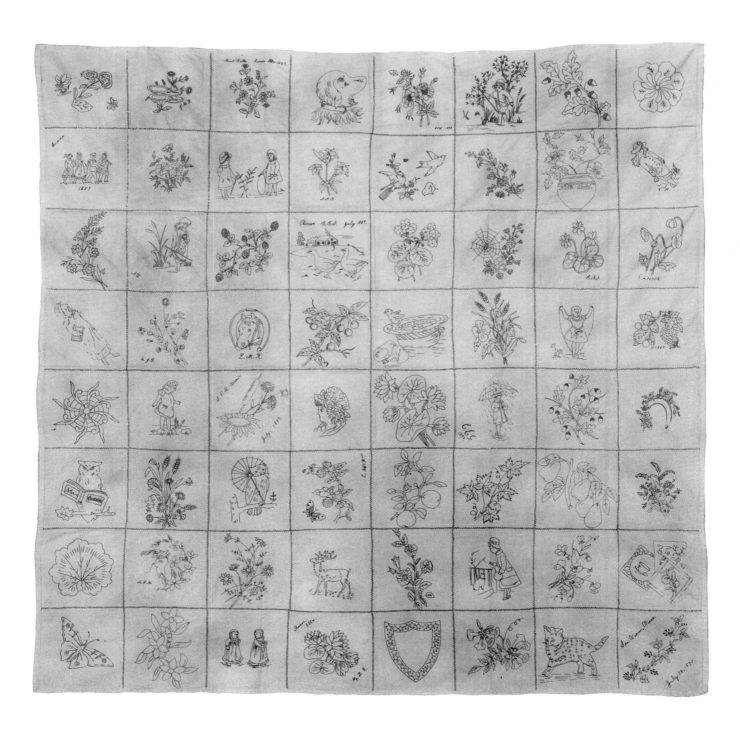

61

Outline work patterns were available in small size, suitable for doilies, handkerchiefs, and the like. In this work sixty-four embroidered squares have been sewn together to form a coverlet. The coverlet employs both common commercial patterns, such as the owl with parasol, lily pads, and spider's web, and some unusual, possibly original, designs. Some of the squares are signed with initials or names and bear the date (1889) and the place (Roscoe, Illinois; see detail). The lower right square, however, says "Sea View, Massachusetts, July 30, 1895." Perhaps the coverlet was made as a gift to an individual who moved from Roscoe to Sea View. The embroidery techniques indicate that the squares were made by several hands.

Roscoe, Illinois; 1889; off-white cotton, embroidered with red cotton; 73″ by 72″

child-land inhabited almost exclusively by the sweetest little child-figures that have ever been invented, in the quaintest and prettiest costumes, always happy, always playful in a decorous manner and nearly always playing, always set in the most attractive environment of flower-beds or blossoming orchards, and red-roofed cottages with dormer windows. . . . No children are quite like the dwellers in this land, they are so gentle, so unaffected in their affectation, so easily pleased, and so confiding."[25]

Greenaway's childlike figures were highly regarded in her own day. Her first successful book, *Under the Window,* was published at the end of 1878. Within a few years, thousands of children around the globe

[25] Austin Dobson, "Kate Greenaway," *Art Journal* (1902): 33.

SPUN IN 1824 BY GRANDMA GRAMMAS

62

Kate Greenaway illustrations served as the inspiration for many outline work patterns. Note the children dressed in the high-waisted clothes of the early century, with mob caps and Buster Brown hats. This table mat was embroidered on an older piece of homespun linen, a fashion that was promoted in women's magazines. The needleworker pays homage both to the old-fashioned styles and to the spinning and weaving skills of her grandmother's generation.

Red Hill, Pa.; ca. 1880; white linen, embroidered with red cotton; 19″ by 31″

[26] *Dorcas* 1, no. 3 (Nov. 1884).

[27] *Harper's Bazar* 12 (22 Mar. 1879): 193.

owned copies of her books, and countless authors were illustrating their own books in the same style. Among her professional friends was John Ruskin, the virtual founder of the Aesthetic Movement, who saw in her work the ideals that he had been preaching. Outline work in red cotton on white linen using figures based on Greenaway's became an immediate international fad. A few designs actually used Greenaway drawings. For example, *Dorcas* printed two line drawings from Greenaway's Almanack in its November 1884 edition.[26] Most patterns are listed as "Greenaway-like"; others completely fail to acknowledge the artist, though they are clearly based on her work.

Outline work did not decorate every kind of textile. It was considered suitable primarily for white table and bed linens, including table mats and cloths, doilies, wall splashers, bed coverings, and pillow shams. Designs were often related to the intended use of the piece. A mat for a carving tray, for example, pictured fish, fowl, and a carving set (fig. 63). A splasher (placed on the wall behind a pitcher and water bowl) might feature a water-related scene, with brooks, swans, children fishing, or the like. Towels were marked with a drawing of the object to be wiped or cleaned, such as a glass or a piece of china or silver.[27]

Mottoes and words were also used to decorate outline work. The fascination with the decorative, practical, and symbolic properties of words came from an earlier era. But whereas the mid-century mottoes

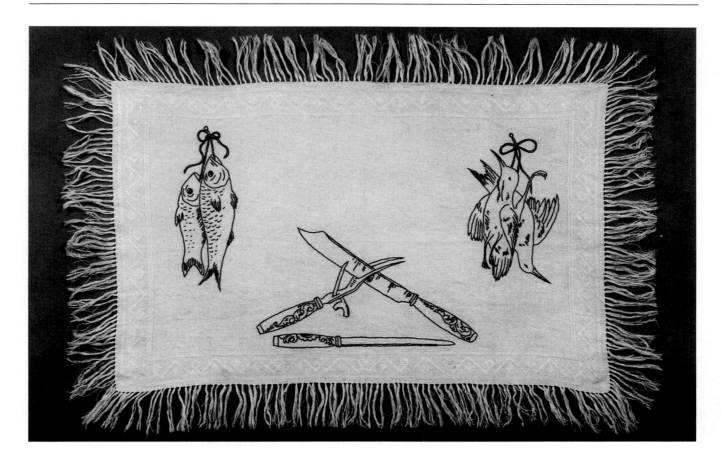

had been mostly religious, the words on outline work ranged from blunt to nonsensical. Pillow shams, which came in pairs, frequently said "Good Night" on one and "Good Morning" on the other. Storage cases were labeled "Collars" or "Handkerchiefs." More imaginative sayings include, "Coffee which makes the politician wise," "Drink now the strong beer / Cut the white loaf here," and "On shining altars of Japan they raise the silver lamp."[28] Often the sayings reflect the sentiments of the era. Consider, for example, the pair of pillow shams that says, "I slept and dreamed that life was beauty / I woke to find that life was duty." Or the towels that teach (in German): "The best prize for any man is a woman who can cook."

Crazy Patchwork

Crazy patchwork, a third needlework fad of the last quarter of the nineteenth century, did not come from Britain, but rather originated in America about 1880 (fig. 64). Most often used as bed coverings, crazy patchwork spreads have been erroneously called "crazy quilts" and studied in the context of cotton quilts. Crazy patchwork evolved only secondarily from cotton quilts and was a fashionable, not a rural, tradition. The use of silk (instead of cotton) developed from the post–Civil War fashion for making silk quilts after traditional patterns. The

63
Outline work suited an era imbued with the importance of "appropriateness." The designs on this finely woven table mat were thought particularly appropriate for use in the dining room. The fish, fowl, and carving set motifs became so popular that each pattern company supplied its own version. The same symbols spread to other decorative art forms; one can even find them on carved mantels and cast-iron stoves.
Northern New England; ca. 1880; off-white linen, embroidered with dark green cotton; 21½″ by 30″

28 Elinor Gay, *Skilful Susy: A Book for Fairs and Bazars* (New York: Funk & Wagnalls, 1885), 72.

64

Some of the outline work motifs in fig. 61 can also be seen adorning this crazy quilt. A product of Victorian America, crazy patchwork combined an interest in oriental art with the new deeply colored silk fabrics of the day. This quilt, which also includes some cotton patches, was made in Kentucky by Miss Willie Love.

Sonora, Ky.; ca. 1890; multicolored silk, wool, and cotton fabrics, appliquéd to a cotton ground and embroidered with multicolored silk; 72″ by 62″

random design probably came from Japanese prints, which appeared in this country at the time of the centennial celebration. The decorative stitches that are characteristic of crazy patchwork were some of the first examples of art needlework to appear in America. Many were illustrated in *Harper's Bazar* in the early 1870s, just prior to the introduction of crazy patchwork.

Crazy patchwork consists of a random assortment of oddly shaped pieces of fabric. The patches were usually scraps of brightly colored silks, but sometimes wool and occasionally cotton fabric, which were appliquéd onto a solid cotton ground. The charm of crazy work came from the embroidery placed on top of the random silks. At the edges of the uneven pieces went decorative stitches in heavy and brightly colored silk embroidery threads. The most common of these was a herringbone stitch. Within the patches were embroidered small motifs, such as cats, owls, and fans, also in brightly colored silk and rendered either in Kensington stitch or in outline stitch.

If crazy patchwork was at first a random and a very personal art, it quickly fell under the control of the same manufacturers who promoted both art needlework and outline work. In addition to patterns for the embroidered motifs and the decorative stitches, the needleworker could also purchase schematic drawings showing the size and shape of each supposedly random piece, with a plan showing how those pieces fitted together. In this particular form of crazy patchwork, the scraps were arranged not on a whole cloth ground, but on smaller squares, which were subsequently pieced together. Not all crazy patchwork utilized materials from old clothing. Many silk companies offered bags containing an assortment of new silk scraps. Advertisements from various silk manufacturers in the *Ladies Home Journal* and other magazines suggest that there was a lively trade in all the materials of crazy patchwork.

Nevertheless, it is the peculiar characteristic of crazy patchwork that all works end up looking random and completely original. One reason is that there were a number of small features that each embroiderer could add for herself. These included the use of embroidered monograms or printed silk ribbons. In addition, the instructions for patchwork were never quite as specific as those for art embroidery or outline work, a fact that encouraged more imaginative productions.

Fancy Work Novelties

[29] Some fancy work crafts were far removed from needlework and thus fall outside the scope of the present work. However, they are important in giving a sense of the eclecticism of the late Victorian era. Examples may be found in most of the manuals cited in Part 4 of the Appendix.

Tea cloths, outline work, and crazy quilts were only three of the many eclectic crafts grouped under the term "fancy work."[29] Another subgroup comprised embroidered or sewn "novelties," including blotters, pincushions, doilies, and a variety of envelopes and cases for collars, ties, and the like (figs. 65, 66). The vast assortment of objects made

65

Adelaide Heron gave directions for this needlework pincushion in her book Dainty Work for Pleasure and Profit *(1894). "To make: roll a piece of cotton in the hand until it resembles the desired shape, then cover smoothly with soft china silk in the proper shape for the article represented, or in white silk tinted with diamond dyes to the required shade." The simple yet effective pincushion was considered a perfect donation to the still-popular fancy fairs.*
USA; ca. 1895–1900; painted silk, stuffed with cotton or silk; 1³⁄₈" by 2¹⁄₈"

66

Mrs. N. DeCelle advertised this blotter in her 1898 catalogue of stamped linen tea cloths and novelties. The cost of the linen was six cents. Mrs. DeCelle, whose store was located in Chicago, also sold Belding Bros. silk. Like the apple pincushion (fig. 65), inexpensive items like this were the mainstay of needlework booths at fancy fairs.
USA; 1895–1900; off-white linen, embroidered with red, pink, and white silk, with red silk bows and insert of blotter paper; 5" by 7¹⁄₂"

indicates how little the late Victorians followed the warnings of Eastlake and others to avoid superfluity of design.

Like the small needlework projects of the antebellum era, novelty pieces were popular as gifts and as donations to charity. Embroidered presents for friends and family were made with greater care than those given to charity bazaars. "It is our experience," wrote one author, "that for fairs and bazaars, articles of useful ornament, made up inexpensively but showily, find quicker sale, and at comparatively better prices than articles of elaborate workmanship and expensive materials, while for birthday and wedding gifts the articles should be as daintily made as is possible for fingers to accomplish, and the best material of its kind should be employed."[30]

[30] Heron, *Dainty Work,* 175.

Counted-Thread Work on Cloth and Paper

American authors were never as hard on Berlin wool work as their English counterparts. Although there was a definite decline in the art form, women continued to work in wool on canvas throughout the last quarter of the century. S. Annie Frost called canvas work "old-fashioned," but devoted eight pages to instructions and patterns. Patterns from Germany, particularly the large pictorial ones, declined in popularity, but smaller patterns, used to decorate baskets, bags, suspenders, and the like, were still printed in some of the more conservative American publications such as *Godey's* and *Peterson's*. The Decorative Art Society did not accept canvas work to sell on consignment, yet the fact that they clearly state this in their rules indicates that some Berlin wool work was still being offered to them. Finally, there are a number of clearly dated works from this era (figs. 67, 68).

Perforated card work also remained popular after 1876, at least in middle- and working-class homes (fig. 69). "Never in the history of fancy work," wrote Frost, "has there been a fashion more marked and popular than the present rage for every description of work upon perforated card."[31] Popular middle-class embroidery journals like *Harper's Bazar* included a significant number of designs for perforated card objects such as wall pockets and needle cases. Subject to the hierarchies of taste, however, perforated work was probably unknown in the finest of homes. In middle-class homes, perforated work slipped from the parlor to the drawing room, and finally to the work room and kitchen. Later, perforated work could be found in farmhouses but not town houses, boarding houses but not private residences.

Perforated card mottoes, though still wildly popular in 1876, were to be a short-lived fad. In 1878, at the height of their use, a well-known decorating manual said, "These cheery and beautiful door embellishments have become so common and deservedly popular that a tasteful apartment is scarcely considered finished without one or more of them." The authors add, however, "We think the fashion (as is too frequently the case with these things), is in some instances carried to excess."[32] By 1880 advertisements for mottoes had disappeared from even the most widely circulated magazines, like the *Ladies Home Journal.* Decorating manuals were particularly harsh. In 1884 an American manual declared, "If mottoes are used on dining-room walls, which is by no means to be advised, do seek one different from 'Eat, Drink, and be Merry,' and other conventional platitudes which are so common in the cheap boarding-houses."[33]

At the very end of the nineteenth century, a new interest in counted-thread work emerged (fig. 70). The predominant stitch was the cross stitch, but in contrast to canvas work, the embroidery threads

[31] Frost, *The Ladies' Guide,* 120.

[32] Henry T. Williams and Mrs. C. S. Jones, *Beautiful Homes; or, Hints in House Furnishing* ("Williams Household Series," vol. 4; New York: Henry T. Williams, 1878), 21.

[33] *How to Make Home Happy: A Housekeeper's Hand Book* (N.P.: Edgewood Publishing Co., 1884), 111.

67

Berlin wool work was not fashionable in the
last quarter of the nineteenth century, yet
many women continued to embroider
counted-thread designs in wool. This piece is
reminiscent of the sampler Margaret Briner
worked more than four decades earlier (fig.
22). In the later version, the thread is not
as finely spun and the colors reflect the new
shades possible with synthetic dyes. Accompanying traditional Berlin wool work patterns
are signs of changing times. Note, for example, the American flag, the envelope, and
the cigar.
USA; 1883–1886; canvas embroidered
with multicolored wool and silk thread;
21½″ by 22½″

68

This pair of suspenders, dated 1890, uses
the bright colors that became available after
the invention of aniline dyes, as well as steel
beads. Some motifs suggest that the suspenders come from the Pennsylvania Dutch
tradition. They may have been made to be
worn with a festival costume or wedding
suit.
Probably Pennsylvania; 1890; canvas,
embroidered with multicolored wool and
metallic beads, trimmed with leather and
elastic; 31″ by 2¼″

69

Punched paper mottoes declined during the 1880s, but were still made until 1900. This motto shows the stylistic influences of the Art Nouveau period. It uses variegated silk yarns in white and shades of gold and brown on a black punched paper ground. A companion piece contains the motto "The Lord is my Shepherd."

Possibly Haverhill, Mass.; ca. 1890–1900; black punched paper with white, gold, and green silk, lined with gilt paper; 20¾″ by 8″

70

At the end of the nineteenth century, the craft of cross stitching spread throughout the country. The fad came from central Europe and is related to the various revivals of folk customs. Unlike Berlin wool work, there was no attempt to cover the ground with thread. Since the grounds were much finer than the canvas of earlier times, women sometimes used checked fabric to assist them with counting threads. This work was made by Rosie Gaugler, the daughter of the "Grandma Grammas" referred to in fig. 62.
Red Hill, Pa.; late 19th c.; blue and white checked cotton, embroidered with white cotton; 16¾" by 24½"

did not completely cover the ground fabric, which was sometimes a checked cloth instead of white. In this form of counted-thread work, the rendering of animals, flowers, and figures was stylized and probably ethnically inspired. The work resembles Pennsylvania German embroidery, but more likely the techniques were introduced into America by new immigrants from middle European nations, such as Hungary, Bohemia, and Greece.

Lace

The last quarter of the nineteenth century saw a renewed interest in historic laces. Many affluent American women began to collect old laces, which they used as patchwork pieces in table mats (fig. 71), preserved with great care in study collections, or copied in modern reproductions. Lengthy books documented the collections and outlined the history of the craft. The elite *Art Amateur* devoted several pages to histories and pictures of lace. A lack of such material in the more popular publications, however, indicates that only a handful of women studied or practiced lacemaking in its historical forms. Instead, four new imitation laces were developed to satisfy the creative urge and the limited abilities of late nineteenth-century women. These were drawn work, tape laces, carrickmacross, and filet.

Drawn work was made by removing certain threads from a solid-ground fabric and embellishing the holes with embroidery (fig. 72). The method was at least four centuries old, having been the basis for the entire history of Italian lacemaking. Compared with the early Italian laces, nineteenth-century drawn work was very much simplified. No attempt was made at pictorial representation. Instead, all the work was purely geometric and decorative. On the other hand, the new drawn work was usually rendered on very fine linen and has a much more delicate appearance than the original works. Drawn work could be used to make a simple line of decoration or could cover almost an entire doily or table mat.

"Tape lace" is a twentieth-century term that refers to fabric made by stitching a ready-made tape or braid into a lacelike configuration. Tape laces are often enhanced with decorative filling stitches placed in the vacant areas around the tape (fig. 73). In the 1880s and early 1890s, the technique was sometimes called "point lace" or "Honiton lace," the former being made from a straight braid and the latter from a fluted or scalloped braid. In the late 1890s thicker tape lace was called "Battenburg" (fig. 74). Many filling stitches developed, for which names were pulled at random from the pages of lace history books.

71

The formation of important public and private collections of antique textiles resulted in a new interest in the history of lace. Some collectors mounted laces for study purposes; others reused old laces in modern clothes or home furnishings. This table runner, along with ten matching placemats, was pieced together from a variety of remnants by a community of nuns in Cincinnati, Ohio. The laces and muslin work included here date from the late eighteenth to the late nineteenth centuries and include needle and bobbin laces made both by hand and by machine.

Cincinnati, Ohio; 1890s; white linen and cotton; 20½" by 45"

72

In drawn work threads from the ground fabric are removed, giving a lacy effect. Embroidery threads are added to make the drawn areas form geometric patterns. In the last decade of the nineteenth century, drawn work adorned many types of table linens, including square doilies like the one pictured here. The spidery quality of the work is complemented by the very fine muslin used as a ground.

USA; 1890–1900; white cotton, embroidered with white cotton; 6³⁄₈″ by 6⁵⁄₈″

73

Home needleworkers rarely made complex bobbin or needle laces. In mid-century, they had worked imitation laces with machine-made net ground. In the latter part of the century, the most common imitation lace was made with strips of machine-made tape or braid. The maker of this cap, or tidy, purchased a ready-made novelty braid that looks like a long chain of lacy circles and stitched the braid to form a fleur-de-lis motif. To this work she added a variety of decorative filling stitches.

New Jersey; late 19th c.; white cotton tape, embroidered with white cotton; 10³⁄₄″ by 13″

74

*In the very last years of the century, heavy
cotton tapes were popularly used in tape
laces. The resulting lace took the name
"Battenburg." Battenburg lace was considered suitable for the borders of table cloths.
Dating of early pieces is difficult, since the
lace remained popular well into the twentieth
century and is seeing a revival today.*
New Hampshire; ca. 1895–1900; white
cotton tape, embroidered with white cotton; 49″ in diameter

75

By the latter half of the nineteenth century, only older and more conservatively dressed women wore white caps regularly. This beautiful example belonged to an ancestor of Ruth Ann Adams Lobdell who lived in Rumson, New Jersey. It is made from carrickmacross lace. The background is a machine-made net, and the appliqué pieces are of fine cotton. The two layers are bound together with a chain stitch.
New Jersey; 1870–1880; carrickmacross lace; 22″ long

Carrickmacross lace received its name from the place in Ireland where the technique originated. Like the earlier darned nets, this lace consisted of a machine-made net ground to which were appliquéd thin muslin shapes. Unlike traditional appliqué, where the pattern pieces were cut out and then applied to the ground, in carrickmacross the two uncut layers were sewn together along the pattern edges (fig. 75). Then the muslin was cut away in all but the pattern areas. It is possible that the late nineteenth-century American craze for carrickmacross lacemaking resulted from the increased immigration from Ireland.

Filet lace used a knotted net ground that formed a very orderly grid of small squares. The pattern developed through the filling of certain

squares with thread. The technique was an ancient one, and suitable to a number of historical subjects (fig. 76). An interest in filet lace increased when crochet patternmakers began to include filetlike designs in their books.

White Embroidery and Marking

"White embroidery" or "embroidery on white fabric" was the late nineteenth-century equivalent of muslin work. In the history of American needlework, white embroidery on a white ground is remarkable for its longevity. Despite massive changes of style and taste, white embroidery

76

Filet work, used in the late nineteenth century primarily for table mats and cloths, looked back stylistically and technically to the early laces of Italy. Many of the designs were copied directly from historic laces. Others, such as this eighteenth-century pastoral scene, were just intended to give an antique feeling.

USA; late 19th c.; white and off-white linen filet, lace, and embroidered cut work; 20³/4″ by 26¹/2″

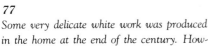

77

Some very delicate white work was produced in the home at the end of the century. However, such work was usually reserved for personal linens and small items, such as baby clothes. By the end of the century, infant clothes, particularly those of the layette, were readily available in department stores and through mail order catalogues. The fact that this bib was entirely sewn by hand, however, indicates that it was probably made at home.

New England; late 19th c.; white cotton, embroidered with white cotton; 9½" by 7"

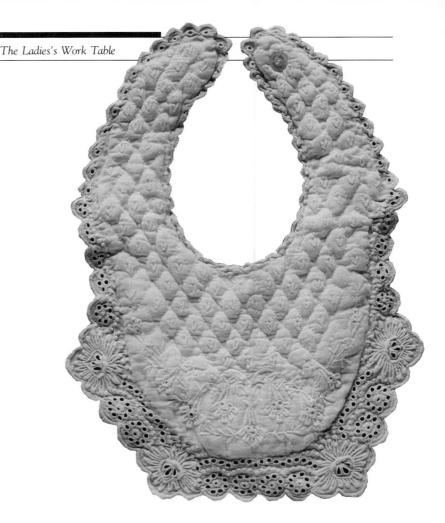

spanned the entire century.[34] The uses of white work and the reasons for its popularity remained the same from 1800 to 1900.

Like the earlier muslin work, white embroidery adorned household linens and children's clothing. The nature of these objects had, of course, changed, so that the embellishments took a new form as well. For example, women's undergarments and a new wardrobe of bedroom attire (which had developed in response to the growing mystique surrounding the female body) had become much finer in texture and quality. Embroidery on these garments, as well as on infant's and children's clothing, had to be extremely delicate (fig. 77). On the other hand, since table and bed linens remained heavy, much of the white embroidery for household furnishings employed raised or padded stitches and heavy, ropelike embroidery threads (fig. 78).

The article to be embellished was not necessarily made by the embroiderer, as it was in muslin work. "Fine linen handkerchiefs with hemstitched hems can be purchased for a trifle at any of the large stores; an initial or monogram worked in the corner with white embroidery cotton or linen floss will change a simple article into one of luxury."[35] Such personal touches helped to make the new mass-produced linens personal and unique.

Marking also survived into the late nineteenth century. Some marking used colored embroidery threads, but the all-white look was

[34] In fact, white embroidery was in use as early as the seventeenth century and lasted well into the twentieth.

[35] Heron, *Dainty Work*, 109.

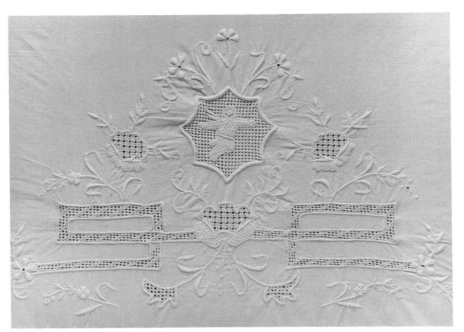

78

The allure of white fabric embroidered with white threads continued in the last quarter of the century. White work was now split into two categories. Household linens, such as this pillow sham, were generally embroidered with heavy white cotton threads on a thick cotton ground. Personal linens, on the other hand, used much finer materials and more delicate designs and stitches.
USA; 1890–1900; white linen, embroidered with white linen; 30″ by 38³/4″

79

White on white embroidery saw a revival in the final decades of the nineteenth century, but the results were much bolder than works of the early century. White work was frequently used on large monograms, which became far more decorative than practical.
New England; late 19th c.; white linen damask, embroidered with white cotton; 28¹/2″ by 22¹/2″

[36] Butterick Publishing Co., *Needlecraft: Artistic and Practical*, by John Q. Reed and Eliza M. Lavin, "Metropolitan Art Series" (New York: Butterick Publishing Company, 1889), 195.

[37] Ibid, 195.

[38] Frost, *The Ladies' Guide*, 73.

[39] Thérèse de Dillmont, *Encyclopedia of Needlework* (1886; reprint ed., Mulhouse, France: Editions Th. de Dillmont, 1975), 245.

[40] Butterick Co. [Reed and Lavin], *Needlecraft*, 89.

[41] Heron, *Dainty Work*, 326.

80

These heavy stockings were probably never worn. They are beautifully knitted and decorated with an inscription: "E F / 1881." It is quite possible that they were made for a country fair somewhere north of Albany, where they were recently found.
Near Albany, N.Y.; 1881; off-white cotton, trimmed with blue glass beads; 20½" long

considered "in the best taste." It also washed well.[36] The custom of adding initials or names to linens no longer served any practical purpose. The letters had become highly decorative, so marking was primarily an ornamental embroidery (fig. 79). It also appealed to the Victorian woman's sense of self-importance. As one manual put it, "It is essentially a womanly weakness to like one's initials upon one's belongings."[37]

Knitting, Crochet, Tatting, and Macramé

By the end of the century, knitting was such a widespread skill that writers were having trouble finding new things to say about it. "A knowledge of knitting has so many advantages that it is almost superfluous to enumerate them," wrote one author.[38] "It is scarcely possible nowadays to invent new stitches or new patterns," lamented another.[39] "Knitted work is as ancient as art itself," said a third (fig. 80).[40] About crochet, which had been known continuously for only 50 years, writers were even less eloquent. "In the chapter devoted to this subject, no attempt at originality has been made," confessed Adelaide Heron (fig. 81).[41]

Rather than alter the techniques or patterns of knitting and crochet, the late nineteenth-century needleworker added variety by adopting two new crafts: tatting and macramé (fig. 82). Like crochet, tatting was an ancient art. The tool used in tatting is a shuttle with pointed ends, which holds the untatted thread. Tatted work consists of knots and buttonhole stitches. Macramé appealed to the exotic tastes of late Victorians. Despite its similarity (in technique, if not size) to Belgian bobbin laces, macramé work originated in the Middle East and resembled the knotted fringe seen on Oriental rugs.

If tatting and macramé were more fashionable, knitting and crochet had a more important social purpose. They were considered excellent pastimes. "No other form of 'Dainty Work' is so conducive to sociability and a general feeling of *bonhomme* [sic] as a piece of knitting

81

A variety of imitation lace was made with crochet and tatting techniques. These could be used to produce simple edgings or larger motifs, such as the butterfly ends of this dresser scarf.

Detail; New England; late 19th c.; off-white linen, with off-white linen [?] crochet trim; 58″ by 17″

82

Mrs. W. N. Seibert of Milford, Massachusetts, made so many small crocheted and tatted samples that she mounted them in a book. (The book is an old ledger that records the accounts and grades of a teacher from the years 1884 to 1892.) Most of the samples are made from white cotton or linen, but some are made from variegated silk threads.

Milford, Mass.; ca. 1895–1900; silk, cotton, or linen crochet samples, mounted in ledger; 11⅝″ by 9¼″

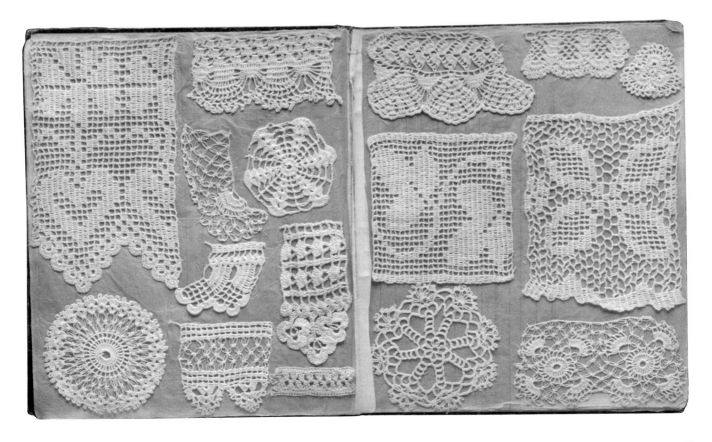

or crochet work. It occupies the fingers, yet leaves the mind free for 'idle converse the while.'"[42] They were also suitable for a very wide segment of the population. "Knitting is really the employment of the millions, rich and poor, old and young, gentle and simple resorting to it for amusement or occupation."[43] But times were changing. In the last years of the century, fewer women spent their days in "idle converse," and knitting and crochet were increasingly considered the pastime of the elderly.

Needlework and Late Victorian Society

In the popular literature of the day, a woman who sewed or made other types of fancy work was either elderly or poor and very often miserable. The last line of Henry James's *Washington Square* has his heroine facing the lonely life of an old maid: "Catherine, meanwhile, in the parlor, picking up her morsel of fancywork, had seated herself with it again—for life, as it were."[44] And compare the situation of two leading characters in Edith Wharton's *The House of Mirth.* Lily Bart, the social climbing heroine, feared poverty, which would mean giving up her apartment for "the obscurity of a boarding house," and "slinking about to employment agencies, and trying to sell painted blotting-pads to Women's Exchanges."[45] Lily's aunt, Mrs. Peniston, who was wealthy, but also in her last years, could sit and crochet without shame.

It is true that both authors deliberately painted a bleak picture for purposes of plot development, but it is hardly coincidental that they used the same metaphor. Decorative needlework, which prior to 1876 had been particularly favored among the upper and then the middle classes, now suited women at all levels of the social and economic scale. As more working-class women could afford to embroider, decorative needlework lost favor among the wealthy and among young women. Wealthy women, living the high life of the Belle Epoque or Gilded Age, spent their days traveling in Europe, playing tennis or croquet, or socializing with their peers. Middle-class young women could attend business schools or colleges, and could consider having a career. Even working-class women had a much wider range of occupations open to them. Many women still sewed, but it was now their choice to do so. Needlework was no longer pastime and duty; needlework was now a craft and a diversion.

[42] Ibid, 325.

[43] Frost, *The Ladies' Guide*, 73.

[44] Henry James, *Washington Square* (1880, reprint ed., New York and Scarborough, Ontario: New American Library, 1964), 180.

[45] Edith Wharton, *The House of Mirth* (1905, reprint ed., New York: Charles Scribner's Sons, 1969), 267.

CHAPTER FIVE

*Ethnic,
Rural, and
Regional
Traditions*

The forms of nineteenth-century American needlework discussed in the first four chapters of this book were developed by and for the urban population of the eastern seaboard. In the first third of the century, wealthy merchant families dominated the world of decorative arts. In the second third, popular styles were dictated by wealthy and middle-class entrepreneurs. The appearance of embroidery in the final decades of the century was controlled by manufacturers catering to the tastes of middle- and working-class consumers. The single, current fashionable look emanating out of the industrial Northeast was both admired and copied throughout the country. Yet the needle arts were hardly uniform in all geographic areas and in all segments of American society. Parallel to the fashionable forms existed a variety of distinct ethnic, rural, and regional needle crafts. This chapter examines three such nineteenth-century American needlework traditions: hand towels of the Pennsylvania Germans, pieced and appliquéd cotton quilts, and sewn or hooked rugs.

Hand towels, quilts, and rugs all qualify as folk art under the current definition: they were inherently practical objects, decorated by artists untrained in the so-called high arts. Their form and function, changing slowly and spanning several generations, were more traditional than fashionable. For their history we must draw our information primarily from indirect sources, such as diaries, letters, and oral tradition.

Pennsylvania German Hand Towels

In the nineteenth century, among the predominantly Anglo-Saxon population of the United States were many individuals who did not descend from British stock and who retained in their daily living non-Anglo customs. Their crafts can be included in a treatment of American needlework because they were produced in this country. And yet their works seem far more at home within a discussion of their own ethnic culture and traditions than within a history of fashionable needlework. As an example of this phenomenon, consider the Pennsylvania Germans and their embroidered hand towels.[1]

The Pennsylvania German hand towel, whose history spanned much of the eighteenth and nineteenth centuries, consisted of a long, narrow strip of white linen or cotton fabric decorated with embroidery (fig. 83). The embroidery, often in red or blue thread, pictured stylized figures or geometric motifs placed symmetrically on the towel. Towels were sometimes, but not always, marked with the name or initials of the maker. At the top corners were two loops for hanging. The bottom was generally finished with fringe or with a fringed piece of drawn or filled work (fig. 84). The needlework techniques were identical to those found in more fashionable embroideries; the seams and hems use typical plain sewing stitches, and the cross stitched embroidery resembled that found in early schoolgirl samplers. The drawn work, however, appeared in Pennsylvania German hand towels well before its revival in urban American needlework. Hand towels deviated from fashionable American embroidery in three ways: their use, the form of their motifs, and their symbolism. All three differences were rooted in Pennsylvania German culture.

Hand Towels and Pennsylvania German Culture

The term "Pennsylvania German," or, more colloquially, "Pennsylvania Dutch," refers to the peoples who emigrated from various German-speaking areas of Europe and settled in Pennsylvania and surrounding states. The earliest German immigrants arrived in 1683. They were followed by a steady stream that lasted until the American Revolution.[2] The people were all deeply religious, many having fled religious persecution in Europe. All were Protestant, but they represented many sects, including Moravian, Schwenkfelder, Dunker, Amish, and Mennonite. Each group retained certain distinct customs but also added certain ill-defined but recognizable "Pennsylvania Dutch" traditions.

The hand towel dates back to the pre-American traditions of the Pennsylvania Germans. They were originally, as their name implies,

[1] For an excellent, detailed study of the Pennsylvania German hand towel, see Ellen J. Gehret, *This Is the Way I Pass My Time* (Birdsboro, Pa.: Pennsylvania German Society, 1985).

[2] Germans continued to immigrate to the United States well into the nineteenth century, but these late arrivals were of a different background. Some joined the earlier established communities, but many moved to the cities and began a process of assimilation.

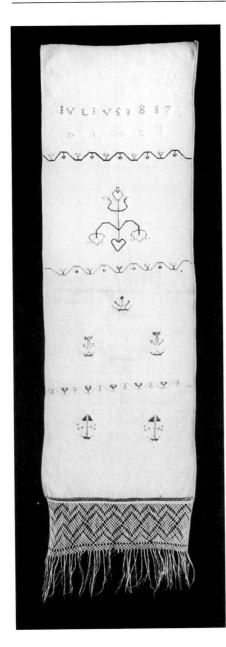

83

This early embroidered hand towel is dated 1817. Note the very narrow width, a feature of early towels. The unsigned work is embroidered completely in a cross stitch in red and blue cotton threads. The three horizontal borders are similar to those used in samplers throughout Pennsylvania. The large motif near the top employs hearts and tulips, two symbols found in much Pennsylvania German decorative art.
Pennsylvania; 1817; white linen, embroidered with blue and red cotton; 45″ by 12¼″

84

Caroline Weidner made her decorated towel in 1853. Even at that late date, she included the same flowering trees found in Elisabet Schefern's towel (see fig. 86). Note, however, that the tulips are much less stylized and more fluid of line than those in earlier examples. The white panel at the bottom is a darned net lace, popular in fashionable needlework at mid-century.
Detail; Pennsylvania; 1853; off-white linen embroidered with red cotton; 57″ by 16½″

85

The same cross stitched embroidery found on decorative hand towels can also be found on other household linens. This homespun pillow slip, one of a pair, is embroidered in red and green cotton thread.

Detail; Pennsylvania; 1830; off-white linen, embroidered with green and red cotton; 17½" by 27"

functional towels. Through time, the amount of decoration grew to the point that they became more decorative than practical. When they were no longer used solely for wiping the hands, they were hung on nails on the inside of a door (thus the two loops on the top corners and the definite direction of the pattern). Like fashionable samplers and marking, hand towels also served a social function: there is some evidence that girls made towels while learning to embroider and while preparing their trousseau or dowry chest (fig. 85).

The motifs that appear on hand towels are the same as those found in urban embroidery (birds, animals, hearts, flowers, and stars all appear), but they are rendered in a different form. In Western European arts the emphasis (at least until the present century) has been on a fairly realistic portrayal. Even in a "conventional" interpretation, which avoided naturalistic shading, the subject was rendered true to form. But in Pennsylvania German cross stitch, as with most ethnographic arts, the rendering of the subject was simple and stylized. Birds are identifiable as birds; flowers as flowers. Even some species of birds (such as peacocks) or flowers (such as tulips) can be identified. Yet their form is geometric and stiff and changes little from one rendering to the next (fig. 86).

Symbolism in Pennsylvania German folk art is not well understood; probably motifs had pretty well lost their symbolic meanings by the nineteenth century. That the figures originally had deep meanings is clear. Some of these related to biblical stories; some signified good fortune, love, times of plenty, and the like. The motifs embroidered on hand towels, therefore, represented a clinging to symbolism long after its meanings had disappeared.

Pieced and Appliquéd Quilts

The course of nineteenth-century quilt making contains two parallel histories. One comprises fashionable quilts, expensive to make and inspired by elite European traditions. Three of these—namely, stuffed

86
Elisabet Schefern stitched her name at the top of this decorative hand towel, but does not give us a date. The stylized peacocks and the flowering trees, all embroidered in red cotton, are very typical motifs in cross stitched towels. The drawn work panel hanging from the bottom contains additional stylized motifs as well as Elisabet's initials. Pennsylvania; ca. 1830–1840; off-white linen, embroidered with red cotton; 52" by 15"

work, pieced silk work, and crazy patchwork—have been discussed in previous chapters. Calimanco, *Broderie Perse*, and Baltimore Album quilts also fall into this category. The second branch of quilt history includes the more folksy, rural craft of quilt making, preserved in the countryside fifty years after it had lost favor in fashionable circles.

Quilt making began as a fashionable art form and became over time a country tradition. The first American quilts of the eighteenth and early nineteenth centuries were made from costly imported fabrics in styles that complemented elite interior designs. Stuffed work, calimanco, and *Broderie Perse* quilts began to lose their popularity in the 1820s and 1830s. They were replaced by pieced quilts made from the

COLORADO COLLEGE LIBRARY
COLORADO SPRINGS, COLORADO

[3] T. S. Arthur, "The Quilting Party," *Godey's Lady's Book* 39 (Aug. 1849): 185, excerpted in Jeannette Lasansky, *In the Heart of Pennsylvania* (Lewisburg, Pa.: Oral Traditions Project of the Union County Historical Society, 1985), 59.

[4] Florence Hartley, *The Ladies Hand-Book of Fancy and Ornamental Work, Comprising Directions and Patterns for Working in Appliqué, Bead Work, Braiding, Canvas Work, Knitting, Netting, Tatting, Worsted Work, Quilting, Patchwork, & C., & C.* (Philadelphia: G. G. Evans, 1959), 189.

[5] S. Annie Frost, *The Ladies' Guide to Needlework, Embroidery, etc., Being a Complete Guide to All Kinds of Ladies' Fancy Work, with Full Description of All the Various Stitches and Materials, and a Large Number of Illustrations for Each Variety of Work* (New York: Adam & Bishop, 1877; reprint ed., Lopez Island, Wash.: R. L. Shep, 1986), 128.

[6] Judith Gould, "Household Hints," *House Beautiful* 13, no. 2 (Jan. 1903): 147, excerpted in Lasansky, *In the Heart of Pennsylvania*, 51.

new, brightly colored roller-printed cottons. These too were probably quite costly unless made from leftover scraps of fabric.

By mid-century, innovations in textile printing had made cotton prints both affordable and readily available. For a few decades (around 1840–1860), pieced and appliquéd quilts made from the new cotton prints were wildly popular among all segments of society. But by 1870 cotton quilts were no longer in fashion. The elite had given them up in favor of quilts pieced from geometric scraps of brightly colored silk or eclectic crazy patchwork shapes. During the era of silk quilts, however, rural women and less affluent urban women continued to make functional cotton or wool quilts. It was during the second half of the century, then, that quilt making truly became a rural tradition.

That cotton quilts were popular but not fashionable can be easily seen in the many references in contemporary needlework literature. As early as 1849, *Godey's Lady's Book* referred to quilts in the past tense. "Our young ladies of the present generation know little of the mysteries of 'Irish chain,' 'rising star,' 'block work,' or 'Job's trouble,' and would be as likely to mistake a set of quilting frames for clothes poles as for anything else. It was different in our younger days."[3] In 1859 Florence Hartley included five pages on patchwork in her handbook, but admitted that she did so only because she particularly liked "genuine old fashioned patchwork, such as our grandmothers made, and such as some dear old maiden aunt, with imperfect sight, is making for fairs and charities, and whiling away otherwise tedious hours."[4] By 1877 S. Annie Frost could state simply, "The taste is one that has nearly died out."[5] And in the early twentieth century, *House Beautiful* declared, "The days of quilting, save at church sewing societies, are well-nigh over."[6] It is remarkable that quilting remained as popular as it did, given the fashionable writers' insistence for half a century that it was out of date.

Design and Techniques of Quilt Making

Quilt making survived *because* it became part of rural tradition. Few books included patterns or detailed instructions, and no nineteenth-century book of any size was devoted solely to pieced or appliquéd cotton quilts. Patterns were circulated by word of mouth; instructions were handed down through the generations. Quilting needed little explanation, for there were only three sewing techniques: the back-stitched seam used in piecing; a hidden stitch for appliqué work; and the running stitch that bound the top, padding, and bottom layers together. All three stitches were basic to plain sewing and easy to master.

The design of a quilt might seem simple, but the quilter faced three design decisions in each work. First, she chose the overall pat-

87

The pattern of this quilt is called Irish Chain. The red and green diagonal bands are formed by a series of small square patches. The white areas have been beau-tifully quilted. Henry Schweitzer, the owner of the quilt, lived in Pennsylvania. Note that his name and the date (1847) have been embroidered in the border of the quilt.

Pennsylvania; 1847; white cotton and printed cotton in shades of red and green, quilted with white cotton; 100″ by 90″

tern. For a pieced quilt, the quilter used a combination of straight-edged geometric shapes; for an appliqué quilt, she could use figures or motifs with curved edges. Next, the quilter selected fabrics, bearing in mind color, pattern, tone, and the juxtaposition of those fabrics within the overall design. Finally, the quilter chose the configuration of the quilting stitches that would bind the three layers together. Even though the technique of quilting is simple, the design of a quilt is a very complex task (fig. 87).

The number of possible overall patterns was, of course, infinite, yet over time certain patterns became more popular than others. These have all been given names, but we should remember that quilt names, like the quilts themselves, are hardly exact. A few extremely popular patterns, such as the Log Cabin (fig. 88), the Star of Bethlehem, and the Irish Chain, became well established and are easily identified. Even these three, however, were called by different names in some areas of the country. In the nineteenth century, the originality of the pattern did not necessarily dictate the value of a quilt, although a certain hierarchy developed based on the difficulty of the design. Log Cabin quilts, for example, were relatively easy to make; the Star of Bethlehem pattern was more time-consuming; and any appliquéd quilt was extremely difficult.

The techniques used in quilt making were also useful for making objects other than bed coverings. Quilting was, of course, an ancient art, and had been used centuries earlier to make clothing stronger or warmer (see fig. 89). In the mid- and late nineteenth century, rural women continued to wear quilted petticoats during cold weather (see fig. 90). Similarly, nonquilted bed linens, such as summer coverlets and pillow cases, could be pieced or appliquéd (fig. 91).

Functions of Quilts

Throughout the century quilts fulfilled two major functions. They were used as warm bed coverings in poorly heated houses, and they served as a major design component of the bedroom. Some quilts were far more functional than decorative. These were often called "comfortables." Others, more decorative than functional, were considered "best quilts," and stored away except when brought out to impress guests, family members, and friends. Between these extremes lay millions of "everyday quilts," which were both decorative and practical.

Quilts transcended their artistic and practical functions. The quilts and the task of quilt making achieved symbolic status. Quilts were tied to family traditions. S. Annie Frost, who had declared patchwork out of fashion, admitted that "it is generally our first work and our last— the schoolgirl's little fingers setting their first crowded or straggling

88

The Log Cabin quilt pattern (made from a series of rectangular strips resembling logs) is one of the best-known nineteenth-century quilt patterns. This typical example has red squares in the center of each block, which by tradition signify the hearth fire. Note that the quilt uses both light and dark color prints, which have been placed to form a secondary pattern of triangles.
New England; ca. 1870–1880; printed cottons in shades of red, blue, brown, and white; 60″ by 43″

89

Best bonnets were no protection against rain and cold, so women fashioned a variety of "bonnet covers." This example, made of very fine brocaded silk, is padded and quilted. Although it is too fancy to have been used by a plain Quaker, both the drab colors and the style are similar to those worn by the conservatively dressed sect.
New England; 1840–1850; reddish brown, yellowish gray, and gold silk and cotton fabric; 10¹⁄₂″ high

[7] Frost, *The Ladies' Guide*, 128.

[8] Fanny Trollope, *Domestic Manners of the Americans* (1832; reprint ed., Oxford and New York: Oxford University Press, 1984), 287.

stitches of appalling length in patchwork squares, while the old woman, who can no longer conquer the intricacies of fine work, will still make patchwork quilts for coming generations."[7] Quilts were made by children for their dolls, by young women in preparation for their marriage day, by expectant mothers for their children, by grandmothers for their grandchildren. Every new generation appreciated the quilting skills of their mothers and grandmothers, and they enjoyed the prized heirloom quilts handed down to them for safekeeping.

Quilts belonged to the social interaction of communities. Quilting bees, or "frolics" as Fanny Trollope called them,[8] were frequent events in many rural areas and served two purposes. First, the sometimes

90

Since the seventeenth century, American women had worn quilted petticoats. In early times, when dresses had a split up the front of the skirt, the petticoat was primarily a decorative garment. By the nineteenth century, quilted petticoats were made for warmth. This excellent example is made from a dark brown printed cotton. The undulating feather design of the quilting was commonly used in the borders of quilted spreads.
Pennsylvania; late 19th c.; brown and white printed cotton, quilted with brown cotton thread; 31½″ long

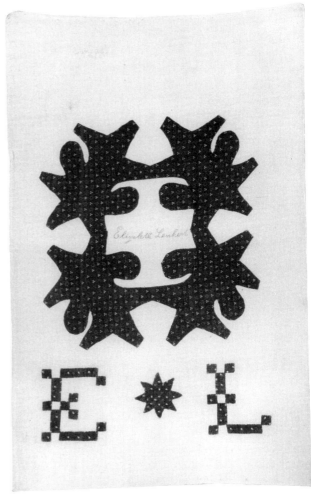

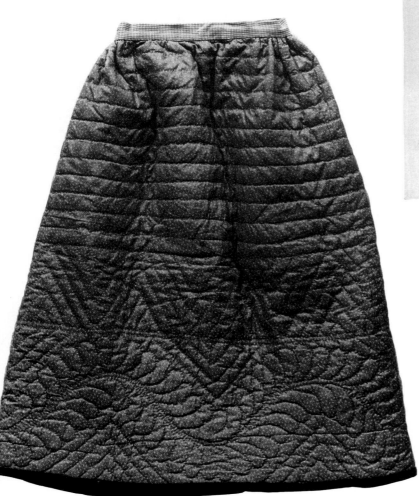

91

Patchwork and appliqué are found on items other than quilts, such as thin coverlets and pillow slips. This pillow slip, one of a pair, includes an odd shape produced like a Pennsylvania Scherrenschnitte (cut paper) and the initials "E L," which are rendered in the style of cross stitched letters. Elizabeth Lenhert, whose name appears in the center of the motif, undoubtedly lived in Pennsylvania, but her name is far too common to be traced with any certainty.
Pennsylvania; ca. 1850–1860; predominantly red cotton print, appliquéd to white linen ground; 26½″ by 16″

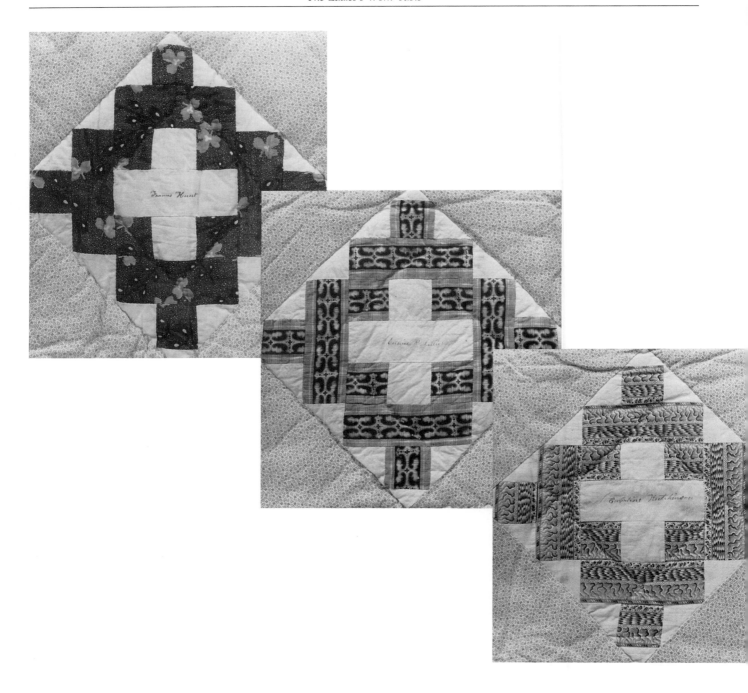

tedious task of quilting a bedcover could be accomplished in short order when several hands worked together. Second, the sessions provided infinite opportunities for conversation and gossip among women who might otherwise lead very secluded lives. Quilting bees led, in the 1840s, to a new variety of quilt: the friendship quilt, usually designed as a group endeavor and made as a gift for an individual or couple (fig. 92).

92

Friendship quilts were commonly made in the middle of the nineteenth century. This example belonged to Mrs. George Calhoun of Coventry, Connecticut. Her husband was the minister of the Church of Christ from 1818 to about 1849. A hand-written tag on the quilt says, "Comfortable given to the wife of Rev. Geo. A. Calhoun by the women of his parish." Many of the names on the quilt (see details) can be traced to the church. The evidence suggests that Mrs. Calhoun received the quilt in 1849 at the retirement or death of her husband.

Coventry, Conn.; 1849; white cotton and printed cotton, in shades of brown, blue, tan, and green; 72" by 71"

Sewn and Hooked Rugs

Nearly every form of American needlework in the nineteenth century originated in Europe. With the exception of Native American crafts, only two forms have been identified as native to this country: crazy patchwork and hooked rugs.[9] Although crazy patchwork was started by and for an elite urban population, rug hooking belongs to the traditions of rural America. Current scholarship suggests that rug hooking began on and near the Maine coast. When the custom spread, it expanded first to other rural areas, such as Pennsylvania, the Midwest, and parts of Canada. Although some urban people eventually adopted the craft, rug making remained primarily a local custom throughout the century.[10]

Recent authors have presented a tentative chronological outline that parallels the history of fashionable work established in earlier chapters.[11] Hand-made sewn rugs of the eighteenth century and the first three decades of the nineteenth served as bed coverings (called "bed ruggs"), and were not intended for use on the floor (fig. 93). Because they were expensive to produce, only the wealthy classes owned them. The 1830s saw the introduction of shirred sewn rugs used as hearth mats, and shortly thereafter hooked rugs were introduced. Rugs of this era were smaller than the earlier bed coverings and utilized second-hand fabric scraps, so that they were affordable to a larger segment of the population. They were probably made as a substitute for more costly professionally woven American rugs or imported Asian carpets.

Rug-making Materials, Techniques, and Tools

The materials and techniques of hooked rugs were simple. All rugs began with a ground fabric, which in the early history of the craft was usually cotton or linen, but which after mid-century was primarily a heavy hemp burlap. To the ground fabric the rug-maker applied spun or unspun yarn (earlier) or thin strips of woven fabric (later). These yarns and fabric strips were usually, but by no means exclusively, wool. The rug-maker either sewed the yarn or strips to the ground fabric (earlier), or pulled loops through the ground with a hooked tool (later). The resulting pile could be left in loops or sheared.

The hooking tool underwent changes over time. At first it was a very crude instrument, possibly designed by sailors. In 1868 Edward Sands Frost made some improvements. In keeping with the inventive spirit of the times, Frost's hook was followed by a number of innovative machines. "The Novelty Rug Machine" was patented by E. Ross & Co. in 1881. It sold for $1.00 and was little more than a latch hook.[12] A similar device, patented by J. C. Rorick in 1884, claimed to make

[9] Rugs were made in America using other methods as well. Woven and braided rag rugs, made in many communities, were not made with a needle and therefore fall outside the scope of this volume. However, we acknowledge that the history of hand-made American rugs presented here is incomplete.

[10] To this date there has been very little solid historical research on the craft of rug hooking. The many books available discuss the techniques and include illustrations of rugs, but a solid chronology and conclusions about rugs and social history are lacking. Furthermore, we have not found sufficient primary material on which to base our own conclusions.

[11] See, for example, Joel Kopp and Kate Kopp, *American Hooked and Sewn Rugs: Folk Art Underfoot* (New York: E. P. Dutton, 1975). Note that the chronology of hooked rugs is obscured by the revival of rug making in the 1930s, when some craftspeople recreated the early patterns.

[12] *Ladies Home Journal* (July 1884).

93

This rug, with its picturesque eagle in the center, is made from lightly spun wool fibers, not from strips of cloth. As in some of the earliest rugs, the pile is embroidered on a muslin ground. The thin backing and the size, which is much larger than most hearth rugs, suggest that perhaps it was used on a bed.

Pennsylvania; ca. 1850–1860; off-white, green, red, pink, and gold wool, hooked to off-white linen ground; 46″ by 50¾″

94

Long hearth rugs like this example are quite rare. The composition is original, but the motifs are found in many rural art forms. Note the relative size of the cats and the horses. Note also the basket of flowers in the center. According to oral history, this rug was made in Pennsylvania, probably about 1860.

Pennsylvania; ca. 1850–1860; multicolored cotton pile, hooked to brown hemp ground; 16″ by 91″

"Rugs, Mittens, Hoods, &c. better and faster than can be done with ten hooks." With all these tools, speed seems to have been the great selling point. The fastest tool was the Pearl Rug Maker, which advertised "Rugs Made in a Day." It, too, cost a mere $1.00, and required "No Knitting or Hookwork." In fact this tool was an attachment for a sewing machine.[13]

Designs and Patterns

Of all the needlework forms introduced in this study, hooked rugs display the most original designs. The reasons were two. First, since rug making began as a rural occupation, there were no early professional patternmakers. By the time commercial patterns were available, the tradition of home-made patterns was already well established. Even at the end of the century, when publishers finally supplied a full line of rug patterns, the majority of rug-makers continued to draw their own. Compare this to the situation with muslin work, Berlin work, and art needlework. Professional embroiderers supplied muslin patterns; German publishers introduced designs for Berlin work; and schools that thought embroiderers incapable of designing promoted art needlework patterns.

Original designs for hooked rugs include pictorial ones that show a scene, a house, or one or more animals, and geometric configurations such as stars and diamonds. Symmetrical floral arrangements and Asian carpet patterns usually signify a commercial pattern. Odd subjects, such as lions, may be original, but were probably inspired by a pattern. Original pictorial designs emphasized their country origins. Farm animals, such as horses, cows, and pigs, abound (figs. 94, 95). Pictures of buildings show old homesteads and farmhouses far more often than impressive brick structures (fig. 96). Even heavily populated scenes document village or small-town activities (fig. 97). Geometric shapes also indicate a rural background. Many geometric patterns were identical to those found in pieced quilts.

[13] *Ladies Home Journal* (June 1885): 6.

95

Horses are among the most common designs for hooked rugs. Many are portrayed in motion, with one leg forward. The use of the horse emphasizes the rural nature of the art form. This example would be far more appropriate in a country farmhouse than in a formal Victorian town house.
Possibly New York State; ca 1850–1860; multicolored cotton and wool pile, hooked to hemp ground; 38″ by 38″

96

Some hooked rugs used existing pictures as patterns. This house is based on a small etching entitled "The Hayward Homestead" by J. P. Hayward. The rug was made sometime after the drawing, which is dated 1888. The family has been traced to New Hampshire, but the building has not yet been identified.

New Hampshire; ca. 1890; multicolored wool fabric strips, hooked to brown hemp ground; 26½" by 39¼"

97

This rug depicts Robert Fulton's North River Steamboat of Clermont, *commonly but erroneously called the Clermont. The picture was first drawn by Charles Balthazar Julien Fueret de Saint-Memin, a French artist who traveled in America in 1810. Saint-Memin's works were later made into lithographs, one of which was undoubtedly owned by this rug's maker. The translation to cloth is not quite literal. The lithograph shows a second boat in the water and includes more of the foreground.*

Near Albany, N.Y.; late 19th c.; multi-colored wool fabric strips, hooked to brown hemp ground; 36" by 57½"
(Photo at left courtesy of the Bettman Archive)

98
Many rugs from the last quarter of the nine-
teenth century were made from patterns,
which were stenciled onto the burlap ground.
This rather static welcome mat (compare the
eagle with that in the earlier bed rug, fig. 93)
probably followed such a pattern, although
the artist remains unidentified.
New England; late 19th c.; multicolored
wool fabric strips, hooked to brown hemp
ground; 21″ by 40″

In the second half of the nineteenth century, rug patterns or pre-
marked burlap grounds were readily available (fig. 98). Edward Sands
Frost is considered the father of hooked rug patterns. From 1868 to
1876 he created well over 750 zinc stencils that were used in combination to make nearly 200 designs. Frost used his patterns to paint the
colors on pieces of burlap. In 1876 he sold all his patterns to James A.
Strout, who continued to market the designs under the name E. S.
Frost & Co. Both Frost and Strout lived in Maine. Strout widened his
market by opening an office in Boston and selling designs through publications such as the *Ladies Home Journal*. A second center for rug making grew up in the Midwest, where Ebenezer Ross sold his rug-hooking
tool and patterns.

99
Among the patterns for hooked rugs are a number that resemble Berlin wool work patterns. Most of these contain symmetrical arrangements of multicolored flowers. Some also simulate mid-century plush work; the fabric scraps have been hooked to form a deep pile, which is cut and sculptured to make the flowers appear three-dimensional. Such rugs are called "Waldoboro" rugs, after the location in Maine where the custom started.
Probably Maine; late 19th c.; brown, blue, gray, and red wool fabric strips and spun wool yarn, hooked to brown hemp ground; 31½" by 53"

Urban Rug-Makers

Rug hooking never became a fashionable, drawing-room needlework form. This is proved by the treatment of the subject in the fashionable literature. No nineteenth-century needlework manual explained the techniques of rug hooking. The art reached the popular press only in the last two decades of the century, and then the coverage was limited to advertisements by tool- and patternmakers and suppliers. The size of the advertisements, the publications in which they appeared, and the number of suppliers suggest that rug hooking in the nineteenth century remained a very limited and primarily rural craft.

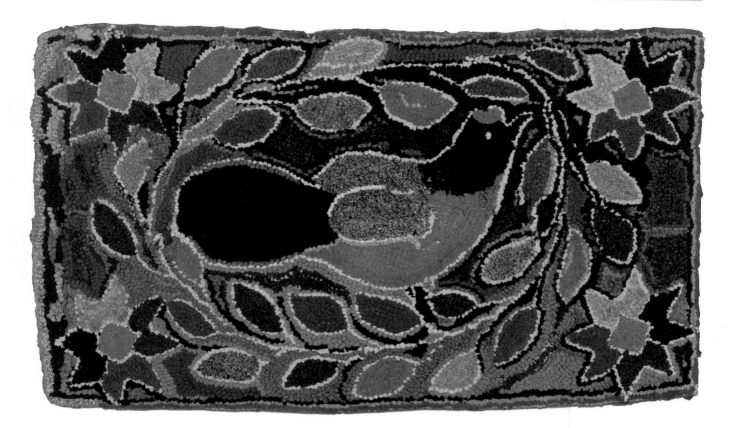

100

Even after lithographs and stenciled patterns were introduced, some rug-makers continued to draw their own designs. This late nine-teenth-century rug displays a robin, depicted in bold red, black, blue green, and brown.
New England; late 19th c.; multicolored wool fabric strips, hooked to brown hemp ground; 18″ by 31″

The patterns that found their way into urban homes included very formal symmetrical flower arrangements and Asian carpet patterns (fig. 99; compare fig. 100). The floral patterns show a strong design link with many of the needlework forms discussed in earlier chapters and especially resemble certain Berlin patterns. Since they were hooked freehand, however, they are far more fluid in line. Oriental rug patterns were used to create cheap imitations of the real thing: "If you cannot afford a Persian rug, or even a very good imitation of one, buy a Ross rug hook, take a piece of coffee sacking, ravel pieces of old carpet for the necessary yarn, and make one; it will cost about $1.50, and per-haps less; if neatly done, it will look almost as well as one that sells at $15 to $25."[14]

[14] Adelaide E. Heron, *Dainty Work for Pleasure and Profit* (Chicago: Danks & Co., 1891), 8.

Our chronologically organized presentation has shown the evolution of needlework styles through the nineteenth century. We have witnessed four distinct eras, four generations. In the first period, 1800 to 1830, the styles are basically those of the eighteenth century. The most common objects were the samplers and silk embroideries made by schoolgirls and the all-white cotton and linen works of adult women. The second era, 1830 to 1860, saw a decline in both silk embroidery and muslin work and the introduction of Berlin patterns for counted-thread work in wool, silk, and beads. During the transitional period, 1860 to 1876, the early Victorian works became large and more extravagant. In the last quarter century, 1876 to 1900, needlework exploded into a wildly eclectic variety of styles and forms—silk tea cloths, outline work, crazy patchwork, and others. With the possible exception of knitting, no needle craft that was present at the beginning of the century was still practiced in exactly the same form at the end.

The evolution, we have seen, depended largely on changes in technology. Many of the various imitation laces used a machine-made net ground that was unavailable in the eighteenth century. Canvas work became popular only after the German printing industry supplied patterns. The height of the perforated card motto fashion occurred only after preprinted cards became available. Crazy patchwork needed a supply of inexpensive, locally produced silk scraps, dyed with bright, synthetic aniline dyes. Silk-embroidered tea cloths could exist only after the development of "wash silks," which could be laundered. Even pieced and appliquéd quilts required large amounts of factory-made roller-printed cottons.

The evolution of style depended also on developments in taste. Twentieth-century authors writing about nineteenth-century decorative arts begin with a strong bias. Many histories of embroidery end abruptly at 1830 or 1840, declaring that no work after that date is worthy of study. Of late, with the revival of counted-thread embroidery, now called needlepoint, Berlin wool work has gained new respect. And with the recent exhibitions from decorative arts of the Aesthetic and Arts and Crafts Movements, there is hope that art needlework might soon find a less disdainful audience. We must remember, however, that within each era of the nineteenth century, the fashion of the day, regardless of its intrinsic merits, was considered in good taste, and work from the preceding era was considered in poor taste. It is from the perspective of nineteenth century taste that we have attempted to view its needlework.

Charles Eastlake, who said with the utmost confidence that "there is a right and a wrong notion of taste" in the various decorative arts, declared that most people will choose bad art over masterpieces if that is what they are most familiar with. "Can any doubt for a moment that he would prefer the most ordinary representations of contemporary life to the ideal and frequently conventional treatment of the classic schools?" he asks.[1] Only after 1850 did Americans and Europeans attach great importance to the concept of taste. The date is significant. "Good taste," at least as it was defined by late nineteenth-century Americans, invariably referred to that which was new and unique, or that which was painstakingly made by hand. The new appealed to the *nouveau riche*; the old to the established elite.

The concept of taste is further obscured by the words "fashion" and "tradition." Fashions are short-lived; traditions survive intact through several generations. For those people who follow fashion, traditional arts are likely to be considered in poor taste. At best they are thought quaint. For those who stick to tradition, it is fashionable products that are in poor taste and, at best, will be termed "outrageous." We have tried to simplify this distinction by segregating traditional crafts into a separate chapter. Quilts, as we have seen, were not fashionable in the second half of the nineteenth century, yet they remained popular in several areas of the country. The fashionable elite would have declared cotton quilts in formal bedrooms in poor taste. The less fashionable would have found nothing wrong with their use.

[1] Charles Eastlake, *Hints on Household Taste in Furniture, Upholstery, and Other Details* (Boston: James R. Osgood and Co., 1877), 1.

Taste, fashion, and tradition are very closely related to suitability or appropriateness, an important concept in the nineteenth century. Each form of decoration and each decorated object had an appropriate place and an appropriate function. White work and outline work were suitable for household and personal linens. Bookmarkers were good for gifts or fancy fairs. Mottoes could hang in family rooms, but not in the best parlors. Furthermore, each needlework style belonged to a specific social or economic class and a specific age group. Samplers were the products of young children. Berlin wool work was accomplished by the middle class. Knitting and crochet in the latter years of the century were the specific domain of elderly ladies.

Suitability leads quite naturally to a discussion of the role of women, for needlework (at least in the nineteenth century) was considered inherently women's work. We have avoided a feminist approach to this study, simply because it is very easy to overdo analysis of the role of women in the nineteenth-century. A twentieth-century viewpoint often causes scholars to be indignant about how women were treated. True, throughout the century a movement worked for women's rights, but it was seldom militant. Yet women made progress during the century. In 1800 there were only two "respectable" jobs for women: teaching and sewing. By the end of the century, the list of jobs available to women had increased tremendously. It was still small by today's standards, but the choices must have seemed overwhelming to the young ladies of the 1890s.

It is only natural that the role of needlework in women's lives would change as their role in society changed. In the beginning of the century, sewing was something that one did because one had to. Some of it was decorative and enjoyable, and some just drudgery. But the drudgery became obvious only in the second half of the century, when new products and new inventions convinced women that they could either shorten the time it took to do dull tasks or, with the purchase of a new machine, avoid them altogether.

A parallel bias sometimes causes twentieth-century scholars to be overly critical of the design of nineteenth-century needlework. We do not always like the works. And we sometimes see the progression of style as a deterioration of an art form. Outline work, we say, cannot compare with the extravagant silk embroideries of the early nineteenth century. But why should they be compared? The silk embroideries were made by young schoolgirls, highly trained in sewing techniques, supervised by a skilled teacher and supported by a wealthy parent. Outline work was embroidered by middle-class women who had no training, no supervision, and limited incomes. But outline work was as highly regarded by the middle-class woman as silk embroidery was by the early nineteenth-century student.

Nineteenth-century needlework was not only artistic, it was also practical. Every sewn or embroidered item had a purpose, even if that purpose was purely decorative. This is hardly surprising at the beginning of the century, when materials and time were scarce. But even at the end of the century, when manufacturers were using words like "pretty and artistic" and "quick and easy," they also emphasized how useful the finished article would be. We have concentrated on techniques, appearance, and social function. We could just as easily have discussed the final purpose. Needlework involves sewing and decorating, but needlework results in an object: a table mat, a bed covering, a garment, a decorative picture. The nineteenth-century needlewoman strove to make decorative and useful clothing and home furnishings. The works illustrated herein testify to her efforts and her success.

Appendix

The following bibliographic list of pattern and instructional books suggests the vast range of printed materials available to the nineteenth-century American woman. We have included all the English-language books that we could find copies of or references to. We have also included a few of the better-known French- and German-language books, which were sometimes translated or adapted for English-speakers. Those available in a modern reprint edition are accompanied by an asterisk (*). Needlework histories are included only if they contain sufficient first-hand information about contemporary methods and styles.

We have not always been able to obtain full bibliographic data for each volume. Indeed, for most of the books included here the exact date of publication is unclear. We have therefore provided an approximate date based on such clues as style, content, and the appearance of the book. When more than one edition is known, the date given is that of the earliest documented edition. The existence of later ones is indicated by a cross (†) after the date.

Part 1: 1800–1830

United States

"Alphabet." In *Metamorphosis, oder eine Verwandlung von Bildern mit einer Auslegung in Versen zum Vergnügen junger Leute.* Hannover, Pa.: Stack and Lange, 1814.

Great Britain

Exhibition of Miss Linwood's Pictures in Needle Work at Hanover Square Concert Rooms. London: E. Rider, 1802.

Exhibition of Miss Linwood's Pictures in Worsteds at the Rotunda. Cavendish Row, Dublin: Wm. Henry Tyrrel, 1806.

A Manual of the System of Teaching Needlework in the Elementary Schools of the British and Foreign School Society. London: The Society, 1821.

The Teacher's Assistant in Needle Work for the Use of Schools and Private Families. London: J. Hatchard & Son, 1815.

France

Celnart [Bayle-Mouillard, Élisabeth Félicie Canard]. *Manuel complet d'économie domestique.* 2d ed. Paris: [Roret?], 1829.

————. *Manuel des desmoiselles, ou Arts et métiers qui leur conviennent, et dont elles peuvent s'occuper avec agrément.* Paris: Roret, 1826.

Germany and Austria

Anweisung, wie eine Stickerin sich selbst, ohne zeichnen zu können, jedes Muster ab- und aufzeichnen, und fortführen oder verlängern kann, mit 50 neuen geschmackvollen Stickmustern. Meissen: F. W. Goedsche, ca. 1820†.

Anweisung zum sticken und illuminiren, mit ausgemalten und schwarzen Zeichnungen von Bouquets, Körbchen, Arabesquen, Desseins zu granirungen und kleinen Kanten. Halle: Dreyssig, [1795].

Die Arbeitsunden im stricken, nähen und sticken. Leipzig: G. Voss, 1810.

Berliner Muster zur weissen Stickerei; auswahl des modernsten und geschmackvollsten für alle Gegenstände dieser Kunst. Berlin: L. W. Wittich, [1817–1833].

Berrin, Emilie, and Jacques Christophe Savin, *Neueste englische und französische Muster zu aller Art der Stickerei.* Leipzig: Industrie-comptoir, [1803].

————. *Gründliche Anweisung für Frauen, auf alle mögliche Art Haargeflechte nach der jetzigen Mode zu fertigen.* [Leipzig: Baumgärtner, 1818.]

Die elegante Stickerin, oder Pracht Muster im neuesten Modegeschmack zum Sticken und Weissnähen. Leipzig: Vetter & Rostosky, [1830].

Erstes Toiletten Geschenk: Ein Jahrbuch für Damen. Leipzig: G. Voss, 1805 (also *Zweites . . . 1806; Drittes . . . 1807; Viertes . . . 1808.*)

Fischer, Dorothea. *Strick Buch: Worinnen nicht nur viele neue Zwickel, sondern nebst dem Alphabet und Zahlen auch viele Zierrathen befindlich.* Nuremberg: n.p., 1803.

Kleines Magazin von Mustern zu weiblichen Kunstarbeiten. Leipzig: C. A. Friese, ca. 1830.

Lehmann, F. L. See Netto, Johann Friedrich, joint author

Muster zum Sticken für Damen. Augsburg: Martin Engelbrecht, 1824.

Muster zur weiszen Stickerei im neuesten geschmack. Regensburg: Reitmayr, 1829.

Netto, August. *Neue original-Desseins für die neuerfundene Stickerei über Stricknadeln.* Dresden: Hilscher, [1809].

Netto, Johann Friedrich. *Neuestes Toilettengeschenk der . . . Strick-, Stick-, Näh- und anderen weiblichen Arbeiten.* Leipzig: J. C. Hinrichs, [1810].

————. *Taschenbuch der Strick-, Stick-, Näh- und anderer weiblichen Arbeiten: Ein Toilettengeschenk für das Jahr 1809.* Leipzig: J. C. Hinrichs, [1808].

————. *Zeichen-, Mahler-, und Stickerbuch zur Selbstbelehrung für Damen mit 48 Kupfertafeln und einem Taffet mit Seide und Gold gestickten Modelltuch.* Leipzig: G. Voss, 1795.

Netto, Johann Friedrich, and F. L. Lehmann. *L'art de tricoter . . . ; ou Instruction complète et raissonnée sur toutes sortes de tricotages simples et compliqués.* Leipzig: G. Voss, 1802.

Neu gezeichnete Muster zum stricken in Garn, Wolle, Seide und zur Perlstrickerei. Pirna: C. A. Friese, 1811.

Neue Zeichnungen zur weissen Stickerey. [Hamburg: Herold, 1820].

Neues Stick- und Zeichnungs-buch verschiedene neue Desseins enthaltend. Nürnberg: A. G. Schneider, [1818].

Philipson, A. *Berliner Lieblings-Beschäftigung für Damen nach colorirten Musterzeichnungen zum Stricken, Häkeln, Tapizerie- und Perlstickerey.* Berlin: n.p., 1809.

————. *Colorirte aus 12 Blatt bestehende Muster, von Antiquen, Vasen und Arabesken, ferner Frucht- und Blumenstücken, Vasen mit Blumen, Blumenkränzen, Laub- und Blumenguirlanden, Vögel, Denkmäler, Landschaften, Rosetten. Bordüren, etc. zum Stricken und Tapizeriearbeit.* Berlin: H. Kronberger-Frentzen, 1804.

————. *Muster von couleurt gestickten Bordüren, zu Kleidungsstücken nach d. neusten engl. Geschmack.* Leipzig: Industrie-Comptoir, 1799.

————. *Muster von Verschiedenen Blumen, Bouquets, Guirlanden . . .* Berlin: J. W. Schmidt, 1803.

Sammlung neuer Muster zum Sticken in Plattstich und Tambourin: Gezeichnet von einer Hamburgerin. Hamburg: A. Campe, [1809]; Hamburg: Perthes & Besser, 1812–1830 (published annually).

Savin, Jacques Christophe. See Berrin, Emilie, joint author.

Silling, Karl. *Grand magazin des plus nouveaux dessins françois de broderie . . . Groszes Magazin für Stickerei.* Leipzig: Industrie-Comptoir, ca. 1800. French and German.

Übungsunden im stricken, nähen und sticken. Leipzig: G. Voss, 1810.

Zeissig, M. C. *Neue Stickmuster zu allen Gegenständen welche in weisz gestickt werden . . . Nouveaux modèles . . .* [Hamburg]: n.p., ca. 1815.

Part 2:   1830–1870

United States

Egelman, Carl F. "Alphabet." In *Almanac for 1844*. Reading, Pa.: Carl F. Egelman, 1844.

———. "For Marking on Linen" In *Copybook*. Reading, Pa.: Carl F. Egelman, 1831.

Gore, Mrs. J. B. "The Royal Shetland Shawl, Lace Collar, Brighton Slipper and China Purse Receipt Book." In *Hand-Book of Needlework*, by Miss Lambert. Philadelphia: Wiley & Putnam, 1847.

Hartley, Florence. *The Ladies Hand-Book of Fancy and Ornamental Work, Comprising Directions and Patterns for Working in Appliqué, Bead Work, Braiding, Canvas Work, Knitting, Netting, Tatting, Worsted Work, Quilting, Patchwork, &c., &c*. Philadelphia: G. G. Evans, 1859†.

Knitting, Netting, and Crochet Work: A Winter Gift for Ladies, Being Instructions in Knitting, Netting and Crochet Work; Containing the Newest and Most Fashionable Patterns. From the Latest London Edition, revised and enlarged by an American Lady. Philadelphia: G. B. Zieber & Co., 1848.

The Ladies Handbook of Baby Linen, Containing Plain and Ample Instructions for the Preparation of an Infants Wardrobe, edited by an American Lady. New York: J. S. Redfield, 1843.

The Ladies Handbook of Embroidery on Muslin, Lacework, and Tatting, Containing Plain Directions for the Working of Leaves, Flowers, and Other Ornamental Devices, edited by an American Lady. New York: J. S. Redfield, 1843.

The Ladies Handbook of Fancy Needlework and Embroidery, Containing Plain and Ample Directions Whereby to Become a Perfect Mistress of Those Delightful Arts, edited by an American Lady. New York: J. S. Redfield, 1843.

The Ladies Handbook of Knitting, Netting and Crochet, Containing Plain Directions by Which to Become Proficient in Those Useful and Ornamental Employment [sic], edited by an American Lady. New York: J. S. Redfield, 1843.

The Ladies Handbook of Millinery and Dressmaking, Containing Plain Instructions for Making the Most Useful Articles of Dress and Attire, edited by an American Lady. New York: J. S. Redfield, 1843.

The Ladies Handbook of Plain Needlework, Containing Clear and Ample Instructions Whereby to Attain Proficiency in Every Department of This Most Useful Employment, edited by an American Lady. New York: J. S. Redfield, 1843.

The Ladies' Work-table Book: Containing Instructions in Plain and Fancy Needlework. New York: J. Winchester, 1844†; London: Clark, ca. 1848†.

The Lady's Self-instructor in Millinery, Mantua Making and all Branches of Plain Sewing, with Particular Directions for Cutting Out Dresses, etc, by an American Lady. Philadelphia: G. B. Zieber & Co., 1848.

The Lady's Work-Box Companion: Being Instructions in All Varieties of Canvas Work, With Twenty-nine Engraved Specimens. From the latest London edition, revised and enlarged by a Lady of New York. New York: Burgess, Stringer, & Co., 1844†.

Stephens, Mrs. Ann Sophia Winterbotham, ed. *Frank Leslie's Portfolio of Fancy Needlework*. New York: Stringer and Townsend, 1855.

———. *The Ladies' Complete Guide to Crochet, Fancy Knitting and Needlework, Containing a Complete Dictionary of the Technical Terms and Characters Used to Describe Crochet and Fancy Knitting Patterns*. New York: Dick & Fitzgerald, 1854†.

Weaver, Jane. *Dictionary of Needlework*. Originally published in *Peterson's Magazine* 1858. Philadelphia: Peterson's Magazine, 1860.

Great Britain

Aiguillette. See Pullan, Mrs. Matilda.

Austin, Miss. See Mee, Cornelia, joint author.

The Balmoral Book of Polkas and Crochet Novelties. London: Groombridge & Sons, 1850.

Baynes, Mrs. Godfrey Cohn. *The Album of Fancy Needlework; or Novelties in Knitting, Netting, and Crochet*. Parts 1–2. London: n.p., ca. 1847.

———. *The Knitted Lace Collar Receipt Book*. Ser. 1–3, London: Simpkin, Marshall & Co., 1846†.

———. *The Young Mother's Scrap Book of Useful and Ornamental Knitting for the Nursery*. London: Simpkin, Marshall & Co., 1847.

Beal, Mrs. *The Berlin Crochet Book: Containing Original Designs for Berlin Work*. London: B. L. Green, 1848.

Berri, Mme. de. *Knitting Made Easy: A Miscellaneous Receipt Book*. London: J. Watson, [1847].

The Book of Braiding and Embroidery. London: Darton and Co., 1850.

Burrell, J. (Mrs. Henry). *The Crochet Gem*. London: Groombridge & Sons, [1848].

———. *Knitted Lace Edgings*. New edition. 1–3 series. London: n.p., [1845–1846].

Chardin, Mme. *The Lady's Repository of Receipts for Novel and Useful Articles in Knitting, Netting, and Crochet*. London: Sherwood & Co., n.d.

Cooper, Marie Jane. *The New Guide to Knitting and Crochet*. 2d ed. London: J. and D. A. Darling, 1847.

Daniell, Emma. *The Crochet Casket.* London: Houlston & Stoneman, ca. 1845.

Dufour, Mme. *Ladies' Album for the Work Table; or Gift Book for 1849, Containing New and Elegant Designs in Crochet Work, with . . . Advice on the Choice of Sewing.* London: Ackermann & Co., 1849.

Eureka [pseud.]. *The Crochet Flower Collar Book: With Point Lace Sprigs; or Crochet de Mille Fleurs.* 3d ed. London: R. Canton, 1848.

Finch, Lady E. *The Sampler: A System of Teaching Needlework in Schools.* 2d ed. London: n.p., 1855.

Gaugain, J. *The Knitter's Friend: Being a Selection of Receipts for the Most Useful and Salable Articles in Knitting, Netting and Crochet Work.* Edinburgh: J. Gaugain, 1846.

———. *The Lady's Assistant for Executing Useful and Fancy Designs in Knitting, Netting, and Crochet Work . . .* 3 vols. Edinburgh: J. Gaugain, 1842†; London: Ackermann and Co., 1847.

———. *Mrs. Gaugain's Crochet d'Oyley,* Book no. 1. Edinburgh: J. Gaugain, 1847.

———. *Mrs. Gaugain's Crochet Miscellany.* Edinburgh: [J. Gaugain], 1847.

———. *Mrs. Gaugain's Knit Polka Book.* Edinburgh: J. Gaugain, 1847.

———. "Mrs. Gaugain's Miniature Knitting, Netting and Crochet Book." In *Hand-book of Needlework,* by Miss [A.] Lambert. Philadelphia: n.p., 1847.

———. *Mrs. Gaugain's New Book of the Most Elegant Novelties in Knitting and Crochet.* Edinburgh: J. Gaugain, 1849.

———. *Pyrennees and Shetland Knit Shawl and Scarf Book.* Edinburgh: J. Gaugain, 1847.

Giles, Mrs. J. W. *The Gift Netting, Knitting, and Crochet Book; or, Knitter's Present.* London: J. W. Giles, ca. 1845.

Hairs, Charles. *The Second Series of the Crochet Collar Book.* London: Faudel & Phillips, [1847].

The Handbook of Plain and Fancy Knitting. Leeds: Webb & Millington, ca. 1845.

Harttree, Miss. *My Knitted Shawl and Tidy Book, Containing Twelve Original Patterns.* 4th ed. London: E. & G. Harttree, 1848.

Hope, Mrs. George Curling. *The Book of the Baby's Wardrobe in Knitting and Netting: A Selection of Receipts for Useful Articles of Children's Dress.* Ramsgate: J. Hope, ca. 1845.

———. *The Knitter's Casket: A Series of Receipts in Ornamental Knitting and Netting.* Ramsgate: J. Hope, n.d.

———. *A Knitting Book for Polka Dresses.* Ramsgate: [J. Hope], ca. 1845.

———. *The Ramsgate Knitting Book: A Few Choice Receipts for Novel Articles Never Before Published.* Ramsgate: J. Hope, 1848.

———. *My Working Friend: Being Plain Directions for the Various Stitches in Fancy Needlework with Hints on Their Employment.* Corrected ed. Ramsgate: J. Hope, ca. 1850.

Instructions on Needlework and Knitting. London: National Society for the Education of the Poor, 1832.

Jackson, Mrs. Elizabeth. *The Polka Book, Containing the Newest Designs for Polkas, in Crochet and Knitting.* London: Simpkin, Marshall & Co., 1849.

The Knitted Lace Pattern Receipt Book, or Examples in Fancy Knitting. Easingwold: T. Gill, 1847.

The Knitter's Cabinet. London: Simpkin, Marshall & Co., 1848.

The Ladies' Work-Book: Containing Instructions in Knitting, Netting, Point Lace, Embroidery, Crochet, &c. London: J. Cassell, 1852.

The Ladies Work Table Book. London: Clark, 1848†; Philadelphia: T. B. Peterson & Brothers, 1864.

Lady's Album of Fancy Work . . . Knitting, Netting, Crochet, and Embroidery. London: Grant and Griffith, 1849.

Lambert, Miss [A.]. *Church Needlework with Practical Remarks on Its Arrangement and Preparation.* London: J. Murray, 1844.

———. *The Hand-book of Needlework: Decorative and Ornamental, Including Crochet, Knitting and Netting.* 4th ed. London: J. Murray, 1846; New York: Wiley and Putnam, 1842†; Leipzig: H. Hartung, 1846.

———. *Instructions for Making Miss Lambert's Registered Crochet Flowers . . .* London: n.p., 1852.

———. *The Ladies' Complete Guide to Needlework and Embroidery, Containing Clear and Practical Instructions Whereby Any One Can Easily Learn How to Do All Kinds of Plain and Fancy Needlework, Tapestry-Work, Turkish Work . . . with One Hundred and Thirteen Illustrations and Diagrams, Illustrative of All the Various Stitches . . .* Philadelphia: T. B. Peterson & Bros, 1859.

———. *My Crochet Sampler.* 2d ed. London: [J. Murray], 1844†.

———. *My Knitting Book.* London: J. Murray, 1846†.

———. *Practical Hints on Decorative Needlework, Containing . . . Directions for the Choice of Materials . . . Methods of Employing Them for Tapestry Work.* London: J. Murray, 1847.

Lorette, Mlle. de. *The Young Mother's Knitting Guide for the Nursery.* Leeds: Webb, Millington & Co., ca. 1848.

Mee, Cornelia. *The Companion to the Work-Table, Containing Selections in Knitting, Netting and Crochet Work.* London: D. Bogue, 1847.

————. *Crochet Collars.* London: D. Bogue, 1846.

————. *Crochet Explained and Illustrated.* London: n.p., 1845†.

————. *Exercises in Knitting.* London: D. Bogue, 1846.

————. *A Manual of Knitting, Netting, and Crochet.* London: D. Bogue, 1844.

————. *Mrs. Mee's Crochet and Knitted Polka Jackets.* London: n.p., ca. 1845.

Mee, Cornelia, and Miss Austin. *The Work-Table Magazine of Church and Decorative Needlework, Embroidery, Tambour, Crochet, Knitting, Netting, etc.* London: D. Bogue, 1847.

Owen, Mrs. Henry. *Illuminated Ladies Book of Useful and Ornamental Needlework.* London: Henry G. Bohn, 1847.

————. *The Illuminated Book of Needlework, Comprising Knitting, Netting, Crochet and Embroidery, Preceded by a History of Needlework, Including an Account of the Ancient Historical Tapestries,* edited by the Countess of Wilton. London: H. G. Bohn, 1847.

Pullan, Mrs. Matilda [Aiguillette, pseud.]. *The Ladies Keepsake: or Treasures of the Needle.* London: Darton & Company, 1851.

————. *The Lady's Manual of Fancywork: A Complete Instructor in Every Variety of Ornamental Needlework.* New York: Dick & Fitzgerald, 1857†.
    See also Warren, Mrs. E., joint author.

Riego de la Branchardière, Mlle. Éléonore. *The Crochet Book.* 4th series. London: Simpkin, Marshall & Co., 1848.

————. *Comforts for the Crimea; or The Fourth Winter Book in Crochet and Knitting.* London: Simpkin, Marshall & Co., 1854.

————. *The Knitting Book.* 5th ed. London: Simpkin, Marshall & Co., 1849.

————. *The Winter Book.* London: Simpkin, Marshall & Co., 1848; 1st American ed. Boston: King & Co., 1849.

Rogers, Mrs. D. *The Regal Knitted Collar Book.* London: n.p. 1847.

Savage, Mrs. William. *Gems of Knitting and Crochet, Being a Choice Selection of New and Elegant Articles.* London: Simpkin, Marshall & Co., 1847.

————. *The Polka Jacket Book.* N.p., n.d.

————. *The Winchester Fancy Needlework Instructor and Manual of the Fashionable and Elegant Accomplishment of Knitting and Crochet.* 3d ed. London: Simpkin, Marshall & Co., [1847].

Stone, Mrs. Elizabeth. *The Art of Needlework from the Earliest Ages.* edited by the Countess of Wilton. London: H. Colburn, 1840†.

Warren, Mrs. E. *The Book of the Boudoir, with Original Patterns Ornamentally Illustrated.* London: Ackermann & Co., ca. 1847.

————. *The Court Crochet Collar and Cuff Book, with Original Patterns Ornamentally Illustrated.* London: Ackermann & Co., 1847.

————. *The Court Crochet Lace and Edging Book, with Original Patterns Ornamentally Illustrated.* London: Ackermann & Co., 1847.

————. *The Crochet Doyley Book, with Original Patterns Ornamentally Illustrated.* London: Ackermann & Co., 1847.

————. *The Crochet Lace and Edging Book, with Original Patterns Ornamentally Illustrated.* London: Ackermann & Co., 1847.

————. *The Point Lace Crochet Collar Book, with Original Patterns Ornamentally Illustrated.* London: Ackermann & Co., 1846–47.

————. *Timethrift; or Leisure Hours for Ladies, Including Instructions in Crochet, Berlin Work, etc.* London: Ward & Lock, 1854.

•Warren, Mrs. E., and Pullan, Mrs. M. M. *Treasures in Needlework: Comprising Instructions in Knitting, Netting, Crochet, Point Lace, Tatting, Braiding, and Embroidery.* London: Ward & Lock, 1855; reprint ed., New York: Lancer Books, 1973.

Watts, Miss. *The Ladies' Knitting and Netting Book.* 3d ed. London: John Miland, 1842.

Wilton, Mary Margaret (Stanley) Egerton. See Stone, Mrs. ELizabeth.

The Work Table and Embroidery Frame Companion. New ed. London: C. Mitchell, ca. 1845.

•*The Workwoman's Guide, Containing Instructions to the Inexperienced in Cutting Out and Completing Those Articles of Wearing Apparel, & c., Which Are Usually Made at Home: Also, Explanations on Upholstery, Strawplatting, Bonnet-Making, Knitting, & c.* London: Simpkin, Marshall and Co., 1840; reprint ed., Guilford, Conn.: OPUS Publishers, 1986.

The Wreath; or Ornamental Artist; Containing Instructions for Making [artificial] Flowers [and fancy work]. Exeter: n.p., 1835.

France

Bricogne, Mme. A. *Album d'ouvrages au filet, crochet, tricots, etc.* Paris: Bureau du Journal des jeunes personnes, 1848.

Celnart [Bayle-Mouillard, Élisabeth Félicie Canard]. *Nouveau manuel complet de la broderie, indiquant la manière de dessiner et d'exécuter tout ce qui est relatif à cet art.* Paris: Roret, 1840.

G., Mme. E. *Manuel encyclopedique du travail de la tapisserie.* Paris: n.p., ca. 1852.

M., Madame la Vicomtesse de. *Album de tricot.* Brussels: Librarie encyclope-dique de Perichon, 1848.

————. *Encyclopedie des dames: Instructions et examples d'ouvrages de mains, tels que tricot, broderies, crochet, filet, lacet, frivolites, etc.* Brussels: Librarie encyclopedique de Perichon, 1851.

Maison Sajou. *Album pour ouvrages au crochet.* Paris: Maison Sajou, ca. 1850.

————. *Album pour ouvrages au filet.* Paris: Maison Sajou, ca. 1850.

————. *Album pour ouvrages en tapisserie.* Paris: Maison Sajou, ca. 1855.

————. *Album pour ouvrages au tricot.* Paris: Maison Sajou, ca. 1850.

————. *Collection choisie des dessins d'ouvrages de la Maison Sajou.* Paris: Maison Sajou, ca. 1855.

Modèles nouveaux de crochet et filet, broderies en soie, broderies anglaises, plumetis, soutaches, laine, etc. Paris: Aubert, ca. 1850.

Germany and Austria

Adnet-Molé, Mad. *Steno-tricographie: Das ist neueste französische Methode stenographischer Musterzeichnungen für Kunst- und Spitzenstrickerei.* Grimma & Leipzig: Verlags-Comptoirs, 1850.

Andreä, Nanette. *Leicht fassliche Anweisungen zu verschiedenen weiblichen Kunstarbeiten.* Erfurt: Hennings & Hopf, 1843.

Hennings, E. See Leander, Charlotte.

Höflich, Nannette. *Die wohlerfahrene elegante Stickerin.* Nuremberg: F. Korn, 1843†.

Kleines Magazin von Mustern zu weiblichen Kunstarbeiten. Leipzig: C. A. Friese, ca. 1830.

Leander, Charlotte [Emma Hennings, pseud.]. *Anweisung zur Kunst-Strickerei zuzammenfestellt.* Erfurt: Hennings & Hopf, 1843–47.

————. *Bunte Stickmuster in Weiss.* Erfurt: Hennings & Hopf, 1846–1847.

————. *Filet-schule: oder gründliche Anweisung alle vorkommenden Netz-arbeiten anzufertigen.* Erfurt: Hennings & Hopf, 1843.

————. *Häkel-, Strick- und Stickmuster.* Erfurt: Hennings & Hopf, 1842–1843.

————. *Häkelschule für Damen.* Erfurt: Hennings & Hopf, 1850.

————. *Kleine Häkel-schule: oder Die Kunst sammtlich Häkelarbeiten zu erlernen.* Erfurt: Hennings & Hopf, 1849.

————. *Die Knöpfel-schule: oder ausführliche Beschreibung von Seide, Band, Perlen und feinen Bindfaden: Taschen, Börsen, Kragen, Jagdtaschen . . . zu knöpfeln.* Erfurt: Hennings & Hopf, 1845.

————. *Modenheft . . . Weibliche Handarbeiten, in Stricken, Sticken, Häkeln, Filetstricken und andern Branchen.* Erfurt: Hennings & Hopf, 1843†.

————. *Näh-Schule; oder Gründliche Anweisen in allen nur möglichen Saumen Nähten der Wäsche, Tapisserie und Spitzenstiche, Damaststopfen, zuschneiden der weissen Wäsche, u.s.w.* Erfurt: Hemmings & Hopf, 1847.

————. *Die neuesten und elegantesten Stickmuster in Weiss.* Erfurt: Hennings & Hopf, [1845–1846].

————. *Vorgeblätter zu Model-tüchern.* Erfurt: Hennings & Hopf, 1850.

————. *Weisshäkel-muster: Als Anhang zur Häkelschule fur Damen.* Erfurt: Hennings & Hopf, 1850.

Leiden, W. *Neueste vollständigste Filetschule.* Ulm: F. Ebner, 1850.

————. *Neueste und vollständigste Häkelschule.* Ulm: F. Ebner, 1851.

————. *Neuste und vollständigste Nähschule; oder Gemeinfassliche Anleitung zum Erlernen aller im bürgerlichen Leben vorkommenden Näharbeiten, sowie des Straminnähens, Nebst einer Farbenlehre für Frauenzimmer.* Ulm: F. Ebner, 1851.

Leonhardt-Lysèr, Caroline, and Cäcile Seifer. *Encyclopädie der sammtlichen Frauen-kunste.* Rev. ed. Leipzig: A. R. Friese, 1837.

Lessing, C. F., and Ida Lessing. *Musterblätter als Vorlagen für Stickereien in Wolle und Perlen.* Cologne: D. Wüste, ca. 1850.

Pauker, Julianne. *Neuestes Musterbuch von . . . Strick-Muster-Touren.* 3 vols. Augsburg: K. Kollmann, 1835–38.

Pracht-muster für die weisse Stickerei. Frankfurt am Main: Wesche, 1833.

Stickbuch: Eine ausgewählte Sammlung der neuesten Muster in weisser Stickerei. New ed. Rostock: J. M. Oeberg, [1839].

Wolle, Marianna. *Sammlung der neuesten, schönsten und elegantesten Touren zu Strumpfen und Spitzen-Muster.* Nuremberg: Bauer & Rasper, 1846.

Part 3: 1860–1876

United States

Guide to Needlework, Containing Explicit Instructions for Every Kind of Stitch, in Plain and Fancy Needlework; Together with Full Directions for Cutting and Making Underclothes; to Which Are Added Complete Instructions in Embroidery and Berlin Work. Boston: J. Henry Symonds, 1876.

Jones, Mrs. C. S., and Henry T. Williams. *Household Elegancies: Suggestions in Household Art and Tasteful Home Decorations.* New York: H. T. Williams, 1875.

———. *Ladies Fancy Work: Hints and Helps to Home Taste and Recreations.* New York: H. T. Williams, 1876.

Williams, Henry T. See Jones, Mrs. C. S., joint author.

Great Britain

B., M. E. (A Lady). *Method for Teaching Plain Needlework in Schools.* 2d ed. London: n.p., 1861.

*Beeton, Samuel Orchard. *Beeton's Book of Needlework: Consisting of Descriptions and Instructions, Illustrated by Six Hundred Engravings, of Tatting Patterns, Crochet Patterns, Knitting Patterns, Netting Patterns, Embroidery Patterns, Point Lace Patterns, Guipure d'Art, Berlin Work, Monograms, Initials and Names, Pillow Lace, and Lace Stitches.* London: Ward, Lock and Tyler, 1870; reprint ed., New York: Exeter Books, 1986.

Delamotte, Freeman Gage. *The Embroiderer's Book of Design.* London: E. & F. N. Spon, 1860†.

Dolby, A. *Church Embroidery, Ancient and Modern, Practically Illustrated.* London: n.p., 1867.

Elegant Arts for Ladies, Comprising Beadwork, etc. London: Ward and Lock, 1861.

Georgens, Jan Daniel. *The Ladies' Book of Needlework, Including Embroidery, Braiding, Knitting, Crochet, &c.: A Series of Sixty-Four Entirely New Designs in Color, with Instructions.* London: L. Hachette, 1869.

Girardin, Madame Marie; Mrs. Eliza Warren; and Mrs. Matilda Mariam Pullan. *Elegant Work for Delicate Fingers, Consisting of Designs for Crochet Work, Knitting, Netting, Embroidery, Point Lace, etc.* London: Houlston & Wright, 1861.

Goubaud, A. *Madame Goubaud's Book of Guipure d'Art.* London: Ward, Lock and Tyler, [1870].

———. *Embroidery Book.* London: n.p. 1868.

———. *Madame Goubaud's Tatting Book.* London: Ward, Lock & Co., n.d.

Hailstone, S. H. Lilla. *Designs for Lace Making.* London: E. J. Francis, 1870.

Philp, Robert Kemp, comp. *Enquire Within Upon Everything, to Which Is Added Enquire Within Upon Fancy Needlework: A Manual of Directions for Crochet, Netting, Tatting, Knitting, Embroidery, and Tapestry Work.* London: Houlston & Wright, 1868.

Riego de la Branchardière, Mlle. Éléonore. Series of books with patterns for crochet, knitting, and tatting. 30 known titles. London: Simpkin, Marshall & Co., 1860–1876.

T., H. P. *The Standard Needlework Book.* London: n.p. 1871; 4th ed., London: n.p., 1877.

France

Dessins pour ouvrages de dames. Paris: A. Simart, ca. 1870.

Raymond, Mme. Emmeline. *Leçons de couture, crochet, tricot, frivolité, guipure sur filet, passementerie et tapisserie.* Paris: Firmin Didot, 1868.

Rouyer, A. *Alphabets variés de A. Rouyer.* Paris: A. Rouyer, ca. 1874.

———. *Le Lilliputien.* Paris: A. Rouyer, ca. 1874.

———. *Receuil de motifs et d'alphabets colories pour travaux en tapisserie.* Paris: A. Rouyer, ca. 1874.

Verboom, Agnès. *La clef de tous les ouvrages de dames.* Paris: A. Goubaud, [1866].

Germany

Daul, A. *Die Beschäftigung des weiblichen Geschlechts in der Hand-arbeit.* Altona: Johann Friedrich Hammerich, 1867.

Filet- und Häkel-spitzen-muster für kirchliche Zwecke. Regensburg: A. Coppenrath, [1867].

Fischbach, Friedrich. *Album für Stickerei.* 3d ed. Leipzig: R. Weigel, 1872.

———. *Stilistische Muster für Stickerei und Häkelei.* N.P., ca. 1875.

Gayette-Georgens, Frau Jeanne Marie von. See Georgens, Jan Daniel, joint author.

Georgens, Jan Daniel, and Frau Jeanne Marie von Gayette-Georgens. *Die Schulen der weiblichen Handarbeit, unter Mitwirkung des Architekten G. Lilienthal und von Marie Sturm.* 12 vols. Berlin: Otto Löwensten, 1869†.

Herder, Natalie von. *Album für weisse und bunte Häkel- und Filetarbeiten.* Berlin: S. Mode, [1870].

Hertel, Louise. *Neueste vollständige und gründliche Anweisung zum Häkeln der Spitzen, Manschetten, Hauben, Börsen, Tücher, Handschuhe.* 4th ed. Hildburghausen: Kesselringische Hofbuchhandlung, [1867].

Höflich, Nannette. *Die wohlerfahrene elegante Stickerin.* Nuremberg: F. Korn, [1843–1878].

Korn, Minna. *Minna Korn's Häkel-buch, neue Bearbeitung.* Leipzig: H. Hartung, 1867.

Kramer's Bazar für Stickerei auf Leder- und Silber-canevas in Vorlagen von angefangenen Arbeiten. Leipzig: Kramer & Co., ca. 1874.

Kübler, Maria Susanne. *Leitfaden für die verschiedenen weiblichen Arbeiten.* Stuttgart: J. B. Metzler, 1868.

Pott, Adolph. *Neue Zierschriften für Weiss- und Kunst-Stickerei.* Hamburg, 1869.

Wilhelmi, Helene. *Muster für Strümpfe und Muster für Socken, mit Anleitung, dieselben zu Stricken.* Stuttgart: Rudolph Roth, 1869.

Part 4: 1876–1900

United States

Arnold, Eleanor. *Miss Arnold's Book of Crocheting. Knitting and Drawn Work. No. 2 Containing Fifty Elegant Designs of Lace, with Full Instructions for Use.* Glasgo, Conn.: Glasgo Lace Thread Co., [1890].

Barbour Brothers Co. *The Imperial Macrame Lace Book: With Numerous Illustrations and Instructions.* New York: Barbour Brothers, 1877†.

———. *A Treatise on Lace-making and Embroidery with Barbour's Irish Flax Thread.* by Mary E. Bradford. Barbour's Prize Needlework Series. New York: Barbour Bros. Co., 1891†.

Beebe, Mrs. C. D. *Lace, Ancient and Modern: Comprising a History of Its Origins and Manufacture, with Instructions Concerning the Manner of Making it.* New York: Sharps Publishing Co., ca. 1880.

Belding Bros. & Co. *The Self-Instructor in Silk Knitting, Crocheting and Embroidery.* New York: Belding Bros. & Co., 1883†.

———. *Souvenir: Hints on Art Needlework.* 2d ed. Chicago: F. Roe & Crone, 1889.

Bentley, Charles E. *Bentley's Catalogue: Part 1 Containing Illustrations Showing Design, Size and Price of Nearly Five Thousand Stamping Patterns; Part 2 Containing Instructions for Kensington Painting, Lustre Painting, Lava-work, Tapestry Painting, Drawn Work, Honiton and Point Lace Making, Iridescent Painting, Paris Tinting, Tissue Flower Making, Embroidery Stitches, Alliance Embroidery, etc. etc.* New York: C. E. Bentley, 1886.

———. *Bentley's Catalogue of Novelties in Art Needlework, Stamping Patterns, Lacework &c, 1884–1885.* New York: Charles E. Bentley, 1885.

Boardman, E. W. See Gay, Elinor.

Bradford, Mary E. *Lace Work: A Handbook.* Boston: P. Mason & Company, 1896.

See also Barbour Brothers Co.

Brainerd & Armstrong Co. *Art Needlework.* Philadelphia: McCalla & Co., 1888†.

———. *A Combined Catalogue and Instruction Book on the Subjects of Silk Embroidery and Popular Fancy-work.* New London, Conn.: Brainerd & Armstrong Co., [1898].

———. *Embroidery Lessons, with Colored Studies.* New London, Conn.: Brainerd & Armstrong Co., 1899.

———. *Knitting, Crocheting, Embroidery, Art Needlework.* New London, Conn.: Brainerd & Armstrong Co., [1897].

———. *Silk Embroidery and Popular Fancy Work.* New London, Conn.: Brainerd & Armstrong Co., 1898.

———. *Table Adornment and Popular Fancy Work: Doyley and Centrepiece Work.* New London, Conn.: Brainerd & Armstrong Co., [1897].

Brown, C. L. *Stitches for Crazy Quilting, Patchwork, Embroidery, Etc.* New York: Stern Bros., 1885.

Butterick Publishing Co. *The Art of Crocheting.* London and New York: Butterick Publishing Co., 1891.

———. *The Art of Drawn Work,* by Mrs. Jennie Taylor Wandle. London and New York: Butterick Publishing Co., 1891†.

———. *The Art of Garment Cutting, Fitting and Making.* London and New York: Butterick Publishing Co., ca. 1898.

———. *The Art of Knitting.* Metropolitan Art Series, vol. 3, no. 3. London and New York: Butterick Publishing Co., 1897.

———. *The Art of Modern Lacemaking,* by Mrs. Jennie Taylor Wandle. London and New York: Butterick Publishing Co., 1891†.

———. *Artistic Alphabets for Marking and Engraving.* Metropolitan Art Series, vol. 3, no. 1. London and New York: Butterick Publishing Co., 1897.

———. *The Complete Art of Smocking or Honey-Combing,* by John Q. Reed and Alice Tully. Metropolitan Pamphlet Series, vol. 1, no. 1. London and New York: Butterick Publishing Co., [1889].

———. *Fancy and Practical Crochet.* New York and London: Butterick Publishing Co., ca. 1898.

———. *Fancy and Practical Knitting.* Metropolitan Art Series, vol. 3, no. 2. London and New York: Butterick Publishing Co., 1897.

———. *Needle and Brush,* by John Q. Reed and Eliza M. Lavin. Metropolitan Art Series, vol. 2. New York: Butterick Publishing Co., 1889.

———. *Needlecraft: Artistic and Practical,* by John Q. Reed and Eliza M. Lavin. Metropolitan Art Series. New York: Butterick Publishing Co., 1889†.

———. *Smocking and Fancy Stitches for the Decoration of Garments,* by Mrs. Jennie Taylor Wandle. Metropolitan Pamphlet Series, vol. 3, no. 1. London and New York: Butterick Publishing Co., 1891†.

———. *Studies in Modern Lace-Making.* Metropolitan Art Series, vol. 4, no. 1. London and New York: Butterick Publishing Co., 1898.

———. *Tatting and Netting.* London and New York: Butterick Publishing Co., ca. 1898.

Cheney, L. Maria. *Lady's Book of Practical Instruction in Art Embroidery, Fancy Knitting, Crochet, etc.* N.P., ca. 1884.

Church, Ella Rodman. *Amenities of the Home.* New York: D. Appleton & Co., ca. 1885.

————. *Artistic Embroidery: Containing Practical Instructions in the Ornamental Branches of Needlework, with Nearly Two Hundred Illustrations and Explanatory Diagrams.* New York: Adams & Bishop, [1880]†.

————. *Home Decorations.* New York: D. Appleton & Co., ca. 1885.

————. *The Home Needle.* Appleton's Home Books, vol. 9. New York: D. Appleton & Co., 1882.

————. *How to Furnish a Home.* Appleton's Home Books, vol. 2. New York: D. Appleton & Co., 1882.

————. *Money-Making for Ladies.* New York: Harper & Brothers, 1882.

The Columbian Decorative Art. Buffalo, N. Y.: J. B. Young & Co., 1893.

Croly, Mrs. Jane Cunningham [Jenny June, pseud.], ed. *Knitting and Crochet: A Guide to the Use of the Needle and the Hook.* New York: A. L. Burt, 1885†.

————. *Ladies Fancy Work: A Manual of Designs and Instructions in All Kinds of Needle-Work.* New York: A. L. Burt, ca. 1886.

————. *Ladies Manual of Fancy Work: An Illustrated Guide to All Kinds of Needlework, Embracing Embroidery, Lace-Work, Knitting, Tatting, Crochet-Work, Net Work etc. etc. etc.* New York: A. L. Burt, 1883.

————. *Letters and Monograms for Marking on Silk, Linen, and Other Fabrics, for Individual and Household Use.* New York: A. L. Burt, 1886.

————. *Needle Work: A Manual of Stitches and Studies in Embroidery and Drawn Work.* New York: A. L. Burt, 1885.

DeCelle, Mrs. N. *A Complete Book on Art Needle-Work,* nos. 1–6. Chicago: Mrs. N. DeCelle, 1894–1898.

Ellis, Hattie B. *Directions for Making French Raised Worsted Work.* [North Sandwich, Mass.: n.p., 1880.]

Foster, Kate McCrea. *Elementary Needlework: A Suggestive Manual for Sewing in Kindergarten and Primary Schools.* Accompanied with 120 Sewing Cards. Boston: Prang Educational Co., 1896.

————. *Fifty Designs for Mexican Drawn Work with Directions for Working.* Boston: Priscilla Publishing Co., [1889].

Fromme, Mrs. Stella Logrande. *The Needle at Home: A Complete Instructor in All Branches of Plain and Fancy Needlework.* Springfield, Ohio: F. W. Fromme, 1885.

*Frost, S[arah] Annie (Mrs. Shields). *The Ladies' Guide to Needlework, Embroidery, etc., Being a Complete Guide to All Kinds of Ladies' Fancy Work, with Full Descriptions of All the Various Stitches and Materials, and a Large Number of Illustrations for Each Variety of Work.* New York: Adam & Bishop, 1877†; reprint ed., Lopez Island: R. L. Shep, 1986.

Gay, Elinor [Mary Gay Humphreys and E. W. Boardman]. *Skilful Susy: A Book for Fairs and Bazars.* New York: Funk & Wagnalls, 1885.

Hale, Lucretia Peabody, comp. *The Art of Knitting: Containing Careful Directions for Beginners as Well as Instructions in a Variety of Knitting Stitches.* Boston: S. W. Tilton, 1881.

————. *Art-Needlework for Decorative Embroidery: A Guide to Embroidery in Crewels, Silks, Applique, etc., with Instructions to Stitches and Explanatory Diagrams, Containing Also a Short History of the Art of Embroidery: Reprinted, with Additions from the English of E. Masé.* Boston: S. W. Tilton & Co., 1879.

————. *Art Needlework: More Stitches for Decorative Embroidery, Containing the Holbein, Punto, Tirato (Drawn Work).* Boston: S. W. Tilton & Co., 1879.

————. *Art Needlework—Point Lace: A Guide to Lace-Work, Containing Instructions in Numerous Lace-stitches, with Forty-four Explanatory Illustrations, and Descriptions of How to Copy and Imitate Old Point-lace.* Boston: S. W. Tilton, 1879.

————. *Designs in Outline for Art-Needlework. Accompanied with Instructions in Drawing, Tracing, and Transferring Patterns, and Directions for Stitch, etc.* 5 vols. Boston: S. W. Tilton, 1879.

————. *Plain Needlework, Mending, Knitting and Darning for All.* Boston: S. W. Tilton, 1879.

Hale, Lucretia Peabody, and Margaret Eliot White. *Three Hundred Decorative and Fancy Articles for Presents, Fairs, etc., etc.* Boston: S. W. Tilton & Co., [1885].

Handbook for Sewing School Teachers. (Teachers' ed.) New York: T. Whitaker, ca. 1893.

Hapgood, Olive C. *School Needlework: A Course of Study in Sewing Designed for Use in Schools.* (Pupil's ed. and teacher's ed.) Boston: Ginn & Co., 1893.

Harrison, Constance Cary. *Woman's Handiwork in Modern Homes, with Numerous Illustrations and Five Colored Plates from Designs by Samuel Colman, Rosina Emmet, George Gibson, and Others.* New York: Charles Scribner's Sons, 1881.

M. Heminway & Sons' Silk Co. *Illustrated Manual of Knitting and Crochet.* Rev. ed. New York: M. Heminway & Sons' Silk Co., 1889.

————. *A Lady's Book on Art Embroidery in Silk with Engraved Patterns.* New York: M. Heminway & Sons' Silk Co., n.d.

————. *A New Manual of Art Needlework.* New York: M. Heminway & Sons' Silk Co., ca. 1884.

———. *A Treatise on Embroidery, Crochet and Knitting . . . adapted to the Use of M. Heminway & Sons' Wash Silks (Oriental Dyes)*, compiled by George C. Perkins and edited by Mrs. Anna Grayson Ford, et al. New York: M. Heminway & Sons' Silk Co., 1899.

Heron, Adelaide E. *Dainty Work for Pleasure and Profit.* Chicago: Danks & Co., 1891. (Later editions: *Ladies' Work for Pleasure and Profit* [Chicago: Home Manual Co., 1894]; *Fancy Work for Pleasure and Profit* [Chicago: Thompson & Thomas, 1905].)

Home Manual Co., *Dainty Work of the Dainty Series.* 3d ed., rev. Chicago: Home Manual Company, 1894.

Humphreys, Mary Gay. See Gay, Elinor.

Ingalls, J. Fred. *Book of Tidy and Point-Russe Patterns.* Lynn, Mass.: J. F. Ingalls, ca. 1884.

———. *Book of Worsted Cross-stitch Patterns.* Lynn, Mass.: J. F. Ingalls, ca. 1884.

———. *Colors of Flowers for Embroidery.* Lynn, Mass.: J. F. Ingalls, ca. 1884.

———. *How to Use Fancy Work Materials.* Lynn, Mass.: J. F. Ingalls, 1886.

———. *Ingalls' Hand-Book of Crochet and Knitted Lace.* Lynn, Mass.: J. F. Ingalls, ca. 1885.

———. *Ingalls' Hand-Book of Darned Lace Patterns.* Lynn, Mass.: J. F. Ingalls, ca. 1885.

———. *Ingalls' Illustrated Catalogue and Special Wholesale Price List of Stamped Goods, Stamping Outfits, Fancy Work Materials, Briggs' Transfer Patterns, Fancy Work Books and Art Novelties.* Lynn, Mass.: J. F. Ingalls, ca. 1887.

———. *Ingalls' Manual of Fancy Work, Also Called Ladies' Fancy Work: A Manual in Artistic Needlework.* Lynn, Mass.: J. F. Ingalls, 1882†.

———. *Instruction Book for Stamping and Painting.* Lynn, Mass.: J. F. Ingalls, ca. 1884.

———. *Instructions for Patchwork: A New Book of Patterns and Instructions for Making Fancy Patchwork.* Lynn, Mass.: J. F. Ingalls, 1884.

———. *Macrame Lace and Rick-Rack Book.* Lynn, Mass., J. F. Ingalls, ca. 1884.

Johnson, Catherine F. *Progressive Lessons in the Art and Practice of Needlework, for Use in Schools.* Boston: D. C. Heath & Co., 1893†.

June, Jenny. See Croly, Mrs. Jane Cunningham.

Kerzman, Marie Louise, comp. and ed. *Twine Crochet Book.* Brooklyn: H. Bristow, ca. 1883.

Kirkwood, Louise J., comp. *Illustrated Sewing Primer with Songs and Music for Schools and Families.* New York: Wynkoop & Hallenbeck, 1881†.

———. *New Songs for the Sewers.* New York: Trow's Printing Co., 1886.

———. *The Sewing Practice-Cloth . . . Directions for Its Use in the Class-room, also for the Individual Pupil.* N.p.: 1889.

Kornmann, E. *Steiger's Elementary Sewing Designs on Practice Cloth with Directions and Suggestions.* Steiger's Manual Training Series. New York: E. Steiger & Co., 1897.

The Ladies' Hand Book of Needle Work. Cincinatti: J. Shillito & Co., 1879.

Lavin, Eliza M. See Butterick Publishing Co.

Lupton, Frank M. *Ladies' Fancy Work. A Manual of Instruction in Artistic Needle Work, Embroidery, Painting, Home Decoration.* The People's Handbook Series, no. 8. New York: F. M. Lupton Publishing Co., 1892.

———. *The Ladies' Model Fancy Work Manual.* New York: F. M. Lupton, 1893.

New York Tribune. *Knitting and Crochet: An Illustrated Manual of Home Industry, Containing Plain, Practical Directions for Making a Large Variety of Useful and Ornamental Articles, Fancy Stitches, etc.* [New York: The Tribune, 1880].

Niles, Mrs. Eva Marie. *Fancy Work Recreations: A Complete Guide to Knitting, Crochet, and Home Adornment.* Minneapolis, Minn.: Buckeye Publishing Co., 1884†.

———. *The Ladies' Guide to Elegant Lace Patterns, etc., Done with Common Steel Needles, with Full Description of the Various Stitches, Materials, etc., Compiled by an Experienced Knitter.* Gloucester, Mass.: Proctor Brothers, 1884.

Nonantum Worsted Company. *The Starlight Manual of Knitting and Crocheting.* Boston: J. A. Lowell & Co., 1887.

Nonotuck Silk Company. *Book on Knitting*, no. 5. Florence, Mass.: Nonotuck Silk Company, ca. 1884.

———. *How to Use Florence Knitting Silk.* Florence, Mass.: Nonotuck Silk Company, 1880†.

Parker, T. Edward. *Choice Collection of Ornamental Stitches for Crazy Patchwork.* Lynn, Mass.: T. Edward Parker, ca. 1885.

———. *Fancy Braid and Crochet Book.* Lynn, Mass.: T. Edward Parker, 1885.

———. *Instructions in the Kensington and Other Art Needlework Stitches.* Lynn, Mass.: T. Edward Parker, ca. 1880.

———. *Kensington Embroidery and the Colors of Flowers: A Complete Guide to Art Needlework.* Lynn, Mass.: T. Edward Parker, 1885.

———. *New Sample Book of Stamping Patterns.* Lynn, Mass.: T. Edward Parker, 1886.

———. *New Stitches for Crazy Patchwork.* Lynn, Mass.: T. Edward Parker, n.d.

———. *Ornamental Stitches for Embroidery.* Lynn, Mass.: T. Edward Parker, 1885.

Parsons & Co. *The Art of Fancy Work. Knitting and Crocheting.* Boston: Parsons & Co., 1888.

Patten, Mrs. Joseph L. *How to Make Home Beautiful: A Treatise on Art Needlework.* New York: Patten Publishing Co., 1884.

———. *Manual of Needlework: Teaching How to Do Kensington, Applique, Cretonne, Roman, Cross-Stitch, Outline and Other Embroideries.* New York: Patten Publishing Co., 1883.

Patten Publishing Co. *Designs and Patterns for Needlework, Including Kensington Arasene, and Most Other Kinds of Embroidery.* New York: Patten Publishing Co., 1883.

———. *Patterns for Needle Work Including the Various Kinds of Embroidery, Lace-Work, etc., with Diagrams Showing the Methods of Making the Various Stitches.* New York: J. L. Patten & Co., 1882.

Potts, A. P. *The Needleworkers' Guide Without a Teacher: Revised edition, Including Also a Guide to Kensington Painting.* Chicago: W. T. Langton, 1895†.

Pungs, William A. *A Choice Collection of Patterns for Needle-Work.* Detroit: William A. Pungs, 1880.

Quinby, W. H. *A Lady's Book on Art Embroidery.* Cleveland, Ohio: W. H. Quinby, ca. 1884.

Reed, John Q. See Butterick Publishing Co.

Ruutz-Rees, Mrs. Janet Emily Meugens. *Home Decoration: Art Needlework and Embroidery—Painting on Silk, Satin, and Velvet; Panel Painting; and Wood Carving.* Appleton's Home Books, no. 7. New York: D. Appleton & Co., 1881†.

Sandford, Lydia Y. *Lessons in Fancywork.* Quincy, Ill.: n.p., 1885.

Shears, Mrs. L. D. *Needle Painting; or Landscape Embroidery.* New York, 1885.

Smith, Ellen Galusha. *How to Shade Embroidered Flowers and Leaves so as to Produce Natural and Artistic Effects: Also Studies in Conventional Designs as Adapted to Needlework.* Chicago: Art Embroidery Publishing Company, 1888.

Smith, Mrs. Albert Burdette. *Practical Lectures on Dressmaking . . . Together with Exhaustive Lessons in Embroidery, Plain Needlework, Torchon Lace Making, Honiton Lace Making, Crewel Work, etc., etc.* New York: Publication Offices of Elite Fashions Monthly and Smiths Illustrated Pattern Bazaar, 1879.

Strawbridge & Clothier. *Crazy Patchwork: All the New Fancy Stitches Illustrated and Plain Instructions for Making the Patchwork.* Philadelphia: Strawbridge & Clothier, 1885.

———. *Dictionary of the Stitches Used in Art Needlework.* Philadelphia: Strawbridge & Clothier, ca. 1885.

Trifet, Ferdinand, comp. *Ladies Manual of Embroidery and Stamping. Giving Full Instructions in Making the Stitches.* Boston: F. Trifet, 1884.

Tully, Alice. See Butterick Publishing Co.

Wandle, Mrs. Jennie Taylor. See Butterick Publishing Co.

White, Margaret Eliot. See Hale, Lucretia Peabody, joint author.

White, Mrs. Livetta. *A Lady's Book on Crochet Work, Giving Full Instructions in All Kinds of Crocheting in Cotton, Linen, Silk and Wool.* Chicago: Western Lace Manufacturing Co., 1888.

Wilkie, Harriet Cushman. *Cross-Stitch Embroidery.* N.p., 1899.

Williams, Henry T. *Williams Designs for Needle Work and Embroidery, Part 1, Worsted Work, Canvas Work, Crochet Work, etc.; Part 2: Canvas Work, Holbein Work, etc.; Part 3, Burlap Rugs, Mats, Small Carpets, etc.* New York: H. T. Williams, 1878.

The Work Box and Needle; or Rules and Directions for Netting, Knitting, Tatting, Berlin and Lace Work. Fireside Library Series no. 15. New York: Coast City Publishing Co., 1886.

Great Britain

Alford, Viscountess Marianna Margaret Cust. *Needlework as Art.* London: S. Low, Marston, Searle, and Rivington, 1886.
     See also Higgin, Louis.

Barber, Mrs. Mary. *Some Drawings of Ancient Embroidery.* London: S. Sotheran & Co., 1880.

Barker, L. *Needlework Patterns by Paper Folding.* London: Simpkin, Marshall & Co., [1896].

Barras, Easton de. *Plain and Fancy Knitting and Needlework.* The Nutshell Series. London: Hiffe & Son, 1897.

Beeton, Samuel Orchard. *The Lady's Bazaar and Fancy Fair Book. Containing Suggestions Upon the Getting up of Bazaar and Instructions for Making Articles in Embroidery, Cane Work, Crochet, Knitting, Netting, Tatting, Rustic Work, and Cone Work.* London: Ward, Lock & Co., ca. 1895.

The Book of Fancy Needlework, Containing Clear Instructions in Embroidery, Berlin Wool-Work, Crewel-Work, Appliqué-work, Netting, Guipure d'Art, Darning on Net, Lace-work, etc. London: Ward, Lock & Co., [1879].

Brietzcke, Helen K., and Emily F. Rooper. *A Manual of Collective Lessons in Plain Needlework and Knitting. For Use in Elementary Schools.* London: S. Sonnenschein & Co., 1885. (Partly original and partly edited from the German of Jules Segorju and Emmy Rossel.)

•Wm. Briggs & Co. *Briggs Company Ltd. Designs and Patterns for Embroiderers and Craftsmen: Five Hundred and Twelve Motifs from "Album of Transfer Patterns,"* edited by Marion Nichols. Manchester. [1880]; reprint ed. New York: Dover, 1974.

C., E. M. [Corbould, Elvina Mary]. *Embroidery and Art Needlework Designs.* London: Hatchards, [1879].

———. *The Knitters Notebook.* London: Ward, Lock & Co., n.d.

———. *The Lady's Crewel Embroidery Book.* 2d ed. London: Hatchards, ca. 1879.

———. *The Lady's Crochet-Book, Containing Over Three Dozen Easy Patterns.* London: Hatchards, 1886†; New York: A. D. F. Randolph & Co., ca. 1879.

———. *The Lady's Knitting-Book, Containing Eight Easy Patterns of Useful and Ornamental Work.* London: Hatchards, 1875†; New York: A. D. F. Randolph & Co., ca. 1879.

———. *The Lady's Netting Book.* London: Hatchards, 1876.

———. *The Lady's Work Book.* 2 vols. London: Hatchards, 1876.

•Caulfeild, Sophia Frances Anne, and Blanche C. Saward. *The Dictionary of Needlework: An Encyclopedia of Artistic, Plain and Fancy Needlework.* London: A. C. Cowan, 1882†; reprint ed., Detroit: Singing Tree Press, 1971†.

Children's Fancy Work: Guide to Amusement and Occupation for Children. London: n.p. 1882.

Cleghorn, Isabel. *Needlework for Scholarship Students.* London: Simpkin, Marshall, 1896.

Corbould, Elvina Mary. See C., E. M.

Cottagers' Comforts and Other Recipes in Knitting and Crochet. London: Hatchards, [1882].

Day, L. F., and M. Buckle. *Art in Needlework: A Book About Embroidery.* London: B. T. Batsford, 1900.

Dorinda [pseud.]. *Needlework for Ladies for Pleasure and Profit, Containing Suggestions How to Make Needlework Remunerative. Instructions for All the Newest and Most Fashionable Kinds of Work, Practical Directions and Recipes, and List of All the Established Work Societies.* 2d ed. London: S. Sonnenschein, Lowrey & Co., 1883.

Fleming, Jane A. *Scholarship Needlework: General Instructions on the Requirements for the Examination.* Leeds: E. J. Arnold & Son, 1895.

———. *The A. L. Series of Pupil Teachers' Needlework Patterns, 1–3 Years.* Leeds: E. J. Arnold & Son, n.d.

Glaister, Elizabeth. *Needlework.* Art at Home Series. London: Macmillan and Co., 1880.

     See also Lockwood, Mrs. Mary Smith, joint author.

Gurney, Mme. & Co. *How to Work Arrasene, the New Material for Artistic Embroidery.* New York: Mme. Gurney & Co., 1879.

———. *Illustrated Book of Patterns for Lace Making.* New York: Mme. Gurney & Co., ca. 1878.

Hartshorne, Emily Sophia. *Designs for Church Embroidery and Crewel Work from Old Examples.* London: Griffith & Farran, 1880; New York: E. P. Dutton & Co., 1880.

Higgin, Louis. *Handbook of Embroidery. Published by Authority of the Royal School of Art Needlework,* edited by Lady Marian Alford. London: Simpson Low, Marston, Searle, and Rivington, 1880; New York: Scribner and Welford, 1880.

Isobel (pseud.). *Plain Needlework.* The Isobel Handbooks, no. 3. London: C. A. Pearson, 1897.

Jones, Emily G. *How to Teach Plain Needlework.* 2d ed. London: Joseph Hughes, 1883.

———. *A Manual of Plain Needlework and Cutting Out.* London: Longmans, Green & Co., 1884†.

———. *Self-Teaching Needlework Manuals Adapted to the Latest Requirements of the New Code.* London: Longmans Green and Co., 1886†.

The Lady's Handbook of Fancy Needlework, Containing Four Hundred New Designs in Ornamental Needlework, Lace of Several Kinds, Including Guipure, Macrame, Punto Tirato, etc., and Also Full and Precise Instructions for the Working of Each Design. London: Ward, Lock & Co., ca. 1882.

Leach, Mrs. Clara. *Mrs. Leach's Complete Guide to Crochet Work.* London: R. S. Cartwright, [1890].

———. *Mrs. Leach's Fancy Needlework . . . : A Complete Guide to Art Embroidery, Knitting . . .* London: R. S. Cartwright, 1886.

———. *Mrs. Leach's Knitting Lessons: How to Knit Fancy and Useful Articles.* Reissue, enlarged. London: R. S. Cartwright, ca. 1877.

Lockwood, Mrs. Mary Smith, and Elizabeth Glaister. *Art Embroidery: A Treatise on the Revived Practice of Decorative Needlework, with Nineteen Plates Printed in Colours from Designs by Thomas Crane.* London: M. Ward & Co., 1878.

Masé, E. *Art Needlework: A Complete Manual of Embroidery in Silks and Crewels, with Full Instructions as to Stitches, Materials, and Implements: Containing Also a Large Number of Original Designs and a Handsome Coloured Design for Crewel Work.* London: Ward, Lock and Co., ca. 1878.

Masters, Ellen T. *The Book of Stitches, with Many Illustrations.* London: Ward, Lock & Co., 1890†.

————. *Drawn Linen Work or Punto Tirato.* London: Ward, Lock & Co., 1890.

————. *The Gentlewoman's Book of Art Needlework.* London: Henry & Co., 1893.

Masters, Ellen T., ed. *The Work Table Companion: Containing Accurate and Full Instructions for Knitting, Crochet, Macrame Lace, and Other Fancy Work.* London: Ward, Lock and Bowdon, 1893.

Morris, May. *Decorative Needlework.* London: J. Hughes & Co., 1893.

Myra and Son. *Myra's Crochet Lessons, no. 1: Containing the Rudiments of Crochet . . . with . . . Original Designs.* London: Myra and Son, [1889].

————. *Myra's Crochet Edgings: First Series Containing the Illustrations and Descriptions of . . . Original Designs of Laces and Borders.* London: Myra and Son, [1889].

————. *Myra's Harlequin Crochet: Containing Full Descriptions and Illustrations of Over Forty Designs for the New Fancy Needlework.* London: Myra & Son, 1888.

————. *Myra's Knitting Lessons.* London: Myra and Son, [1889].

Needlecraft Limited. *The Modern Book of Cross Stitch Designs.* Manchester: Needlecraft Limited, n.d.

Riego de la Branchardière, Mlle. Eáléonore. *The Irish Lace Instructor. Containing Original Designs for Spanish Points, &c.* London: n.p., 1886.

————. *Winter Book for 1886, Containing New Stitches in Needlework with Full Illustrated Instructions for the Most Fashionable Dress Trimmings.* London: Simpkin, Marshall & Co., 1886.

Rosevear E. *A Manual of Needlework, Knitting and Cutting Out for Evening, Continuation Schools.* London: Macmillan & Co., 1894†.

————. *Textbook of Needlework, Knitting, and Cutting Out.* London: n.p., 1897.

Stanley, K. *Needlework and Cutting Out: Being Hints, &c. for the Use of Teachers.* London: n.p., 1883†.

Sylvia [pseud.]. *The Lady's Guide to Home Dressmaking and Millinery.* London: Ward, Lock and Co., 1883.

————. *Sylvia's Berlin Work Instructions.* London: Ward, Lock & Co., n.d.

————. *Sylvia's Book of Church Embroidery: A Manual of Instructions for Beginners.* London: Ward, Lock & Co., n.d.

————. *Sylvia's Book of Macramé Lace, Containing Illustrations of Many New and Original Designs, With Complete Instructions for Working, a Choice of Materials and Suggestions for Their Adaptation.* London: Ward, Lock & Co., 1883.

————. *Sylvia's Book of Monograms and Initials for Embroidery.* London: Ward, Lock & Co., 1887.

————. *Sylvia's Book of New Designs in Knitting, Netting and Crochet, Containing a Selection of Useful Articles in Crochet, Knitting, Tatting, and Netting, with Minute Details.* London: Ward, Lock & Co., [1881].

————. *Sylvia's Book of Ornamental Needlework, Containing Illustrations of Various New Designs.* London: Ward, Lock & Co., 1883.

————. *Sylvia's Crochet Book.* London: Ward, Lock & Co., ca 1879.

Sylvia's Illustrated Embroidery Book, Containing . . . Ornamental Designs in Broderie Anglaise, Appliqué, Cross Stitch, and the New Holbein Work. London: Ward, Lock & Co., 1879.

T., H. P. *Plain Cutting Out for Standards IV, V and VI as Now Required by the Government Education Department.* London: n.p., 1877.

————. *Plain Knitting and Mending, in Six Standards.* London: n.p. 1877.

————. *Plain Needlework: Arranged in Six Standards as Required by the Educational Code of 1877.* London: n.p., 1877.

————. *The Standard Needlework Book.* London: n.p., 1871†.

Townsend, W. G. Paulson; Louisa F. Pesel; et al. *Embroidery; or The Craft of the Needle.* Preface by Walter Crane. London: Truslove, Hanson & Comba, 1899†.

Turner, Miss. *Practical Hints on the Revived Art of Crewel and Silk Embroidery.* 3d ed. London: n.p., 1877.

W., C. R. *Embroidery and Art Needlework Designs.* London: Hatchards, [1879].

Walker, Agnes. *Manual of Needlework and Cutting Out. Specially Adapted for Teachers of Sewing, Students and Pupil-teachers.* London: Blackie & Son, 1897†.

Warleigh, Henrietta. *Full Directions and Scales for Knitting Edgings, Circles, Insertions, Repeating Designs, etc.: Over 160 Patterns, Sizes and Sorts.* London: Simpkin, Marshall & Co. [1898].

————. *Full Directions and Scales for Knitting Gloves, Babies' Things, Capes, Petticoats, etc.: Over 170 Patterns, Sizes and Sorts.* London: Simpkin, Marshall, Hamilton, Kent & Co., [1898].

————. *Full Directions and Scales for Knitting Socks, Stockings, Babies', Doll's and Seamen's Things, etc.* London: Simpkin, Marshall, Hamilton, Kent & Co., [1898].

Warren, Miss J. W. *Practical School Needlework.* London: J. Hughes & Co., 1893.

Weldon, C. E. *Weldon's Practical Needlework: Comprising How to Knit . . . How to Crochet . . . How to Make Macrame Lace, How to Arrange Patchwork.* Vols. 1–12. London: Weldon & Co., ca. 1895.

Zeta. *Crewel Work: Fifteen Designs with Complete Instructions.* London: n.p. 1879.

France

Alq, Louise d' [pseud.]. *Les ouvrages de main en famille: Le tricot, le filet, le filet-guipure, le crochet, la frivolité, le travail au métier.* 2d ed. Paris: François Ebhart, 1877.

Boulanger, Mme. Edith. *Leçons d'ouvrages de dames; ou, manuel du travail à l'aiguille.* Paris: L. Boulanger, 1881.

Champeaux, Alfred de. *Dessins et modèles: Les arts du tissu: Étoffes, tapisseries, broderies, dentelles, reliures.* Paris: J. Rouam, [1892].

De-Chagrin, K. *Modèles pour la broderie au plumetis, composées par le professeur de dessin aux écoles des demoiselles de la Société impériale des dames patriotes.* St. Petersburg: A. F. Marcks, [1895]. Russian and French.

Ducerceau and Marot. *Ornaments pour broderies.* Paris: n.p., 1896.

Dufaux de la Jonchère, Ermance. *Le travail manuel: Traité pratique de la broderie et de la tapisserie.* Paris: Garnier, 1894.

Fraipont, Gustave. *L'art dans les travaux à l'aiguille: Ouvrage orné de trente-neuf dessins inedits de l'auteur et d'un album de trente-deux doubles planches en couleurs donnant des specimens de tissus de toutes les epoques.* Paris: H. Laurens, 1897.

Giroux, Mme. A. *Manual d'examen pour l'enseignement de la coupe et de l'assemblage des vêtements de femmes et d'enfants.* Paris: Hachette et Cie., 1881.

———. *Traité de la coupe et de l'assemblage des vêtements de femmes et d'enfants.* Paris: Hachette et Cie., 1891.

Sajou, Maison. *Album de divers travaux executés sur la fourche à franges, deuxieme.* Paris: Maison Sajou, n.d.

———. *Album de modèles de tricot, avec explications.* Paris: Maison Sajou, 1881.

———. *Albums pour ouvrages au tricot.* Paris: Maison Sajou, [1886].

———. *Album pour ouvrages de travaux à la fourche.* New ed. Paris: Maison Sajou, [1883].

Müntz, Eugène. *Tapisseries, broderies et dentelles: Recueil de modeles anciens et modernes.* Paris: Librarie de l'Art, 1890.

Petit cours de travaux manuels (tricot-couture coupe et confection) à l'usage des jeunes filles, par une institutrice publique. Lille: E. Robbe, 1897.

Germany, Austria, Etc.

Album für altdeutsche Leinen-stickerei und Stickerei auf Java-canevas. Leipzig: Kramer, [1878].

Anker, Erna. *Muster-album für Häkelarbeiten.* Leipzig: H. Barsdorf, 1887.

Bach, Frau Emilie. *Muster Stilvoller Handarbeiten.* 2 vols. Vienna: R. v. Walheim, 1879†.

———. *Neue Muster in altem Stil: New Patterns in Old Style: Ouvrages nouveaux de style ancien.* Dornach: T. de Dillmont, [1894].

Burchard, A. *Musterblätter für Kreuzstichstickereien.* Berlin: Winkelmann & Söhne, [1892].

Clasen-Schmid, Mathilde. *Musterbuch für Frauenarbeiten, mit erklärendem Text.* 2 vols. Leipzig: Hoffmann & Ohnstein, 1881.

*Dillmont, Thérèse de. *Encyclopedia of Needlework.* Mulhouse: T. de Dillmont, 1886†; reprint ed., Philadelphia: Running Press, 1972.

———. *D. M. C. Library series, including over 36 volumes of patterns and instructions in embroidery, knitting, crochet, and lace making, published in French, German, English, Italian, Spanish, and Russian.* Mulhouse: T. de Dillmont, ca. 1890.

Fiscbach, Friedrich. *Stickerei-album des Bazar.* Berlin: Bazar-Actien-Gesellschaft, 1897†.

Frauberger, F. *Handbuch der Spitzenkunde: Technisches und Geschichtliches über die Näh-, Klöppel- und Maschinenspitzen.* Leipzig: E. A. Seemann, 1894.

Freimann, Jenny. *Muster-album von Kreuzstichmonogrammen.* [Berlin; n.p., 1890].

Froehlich, W. *Neue farbige Kreuzstichmuster.* Berlin: E. Wasmuth, 1888.

Georgens, Jan Daniel. *Das Häkeln: Mit einer Ornamentik aus drei Jahrhunderten . . . unter Mitwirkung von Maria Sturm und Florentine Sturm.* 3d ed. Leipzig: Oscar. Schneider, [1888].

———. *Das Stricken: Mit einer Ornamentik aus drei Jahrhunderten . . . unter Mitwirkung von Marie Sturm . . . und Florentine Sturm.* 4th ed. Leipzig: Oscar Schneider, 1882–1885.

Grosse Stickmuster-Sammlung. Auswahl der schönsten Muster aus J. Petersen-Wagner's Stickmuster-Zeitung, Vorlagen für Bunt und Weisstickerei, Muster für Flachstickerei. Leipzig: P. Hobbing, 1892.

Hagen, Luise. *Die Nadel Künste: Theoretische Leitfaden der Künsthandarbeiten.* Berlin: Schriftenvertriebsanstalt, 1897.

Hakel- und Stickmuster der Modenwelt Sammlung. Berlin: E. Lipperheide, 1897.

Helbing, K. *Spitzen-Album.* Vienna: R. V. Waldheim, [1877].

Hirth, Georg. *Album für Frauen-arbeit enthaltend klassische Motive für Weisstickerei, Bunt-, Gold-, und Applikationsstickerei, Spitzen-, Verschnürungs- und Knüpfarbeit, sowie Weberei, Passementrie und Stoffbemalung.* Munich and Leipzig: Georg Hirth, 1880.

Hochfelden, Frau Brigitta Langerfeldt, ed. *Ebhardt's Handarbeiten: Anleitung zum Erlernen der verschiedenen Handarbeits-techniken.* 7 vols. Berlin: Franz Ebhardt & Co., [1894–1895].

———. *Das Filet und das Filettopfen.* Berlin: Franz Ebhardt & Co., [1889].

———. *Die Gabelhäkelei: Anleitung zur Anfertigung zahlreicher hübscher und leichter Muster.* Berlin: Franz Ebhardt & Co., [1885].

———. *Das Häkeln: Ausführliche Anleitung zur Erlernung der Häkelarbeit und Handbuch der gesammten Häkelkunst.* Berlin: Franz Ebhardt & Co., [1892].

Jamnig, C., and A. Richter. *Die Technik der geklöppelten Spitze: Original-entwürfe und Ausführingen.* Vienna: Spielhagen & Schurich, [1886].

Kabilka, P., and J. Kabilka. *Kreuztich-Muster im neuen Stil.* Vienna: Verlag der "Wiener Mode," [1900].

Karagodina, M. *Kreuzstichmuster.* Odessa: n.p. 1880.

Kramer's Handbuch für weibliche Handarbeiten. 3d ed. Leipzig: Kramer & Co., [1877].

Kühn, Heinrich. *Album moderner stickmuster . . . für ornamentale Stickereien.* Berlin: A. Seydel, [1880].

Lilly [pseud.]. *Lilly's Stickmusteralbum . . . entworfen und gezeichnet in der Gewerbeschule für Mädchen in Hamburg.* Harburg a. d. Elbe: Gustav Elkan, [1879].

———. *Lilly's Stickmusterbüchlein: Eine Sammlung in Farben ausgeführter stylvoller Stickmuster bearbeitet von den Lehrerinnen der Hamburger Gewerbeschule.* Harburg a. d. Elbe: Gustav Elkan, [1879].

Lipperheide, Frieda. *Die decorative Kunst-Stickerei.* Vols. 1–4. Berlin: Franz Lipperheide, 1890.

Manteuffel, Erna von. *Album altdeutscher Leinenstickerei.* Harburg a. d. Elbe: G. Elkan, [1883].

———. *Filet-guipure-album: Eine Sammlung stilvoller praktisch ausgeführter Originalmuster.* Harburg a. d. Elbe: G. Elkan, [1881].

———. *Monogramm-album sechshundert stilvoll verschlungene Buchstaben für Plattstich-stickerei.* Harburg a. d. Elbe: G. Elkan, [1881].

Modene Stickereien: Eine Auswahl moderner Stickerei-Arbeiten in jeder Technik, sowie neuzeitlicher Entwürfe hervorragender Künstler und Künstlerinnen. Darmstadt: A. Koch, 1900.

Musterbucher fur weibliche Handarbeit: Heraus gegaben von der Redaction der Modenwelt. 1st ed. Berlin: F. Lipperheide, 1882.

Neue Häkelmappe: Eine Anzahl schöner Häkelmuster nebst genauer Beschreibung. Leipzig: Kramer & Co., [1879].

Neue praktische Strickschule: vollständige Anleitung zum Erlernen des Strickens mit . . . Strickmustern. Leipzig: Kramer & Co., [1879].

Oppenheim, Guido. *Neues Stick-musterbuch.* Frankfurt am Main: Gottlieb & Müller, 1878.

Rasmussen, Sara. *Klöppelbuch: Eine Anleitung zum Selbstunterricht im Spitzenklöppeln.* Copenhagen: A. F. Höst, 1884.

Rausche-Rauss, Frieda. *Häckel-vorlagen für Schule und Haus.* Pforzheim: Otto Riecker, [1892].

Redtenbacher, M. *Farbige Stickerei-vorlagen.* Karlsruhe: J. Veith, 1891†.

Reinle, Sophie. *Neue Häkel-vorlagen.* Konstanz: J. A. Pecht, [1892].

Saint-George, Amalie von. *Die Kunst der Goldstickerei: nebst einer Anleitung zur Verwendung der Goldstickerei in Verbindung mit Application.* Vienna: Verlag der "Wiener Mode," [1896].

Scheffers, A. *Neue Muster-vorlagen für farbige Kreuzsticharbeiten.* Leipzig: J. M. Gebhardt, 1887.

Schinnerer, L. *Lehrgänge für Weissstickerei und Knüpfarbeit nebst einem Anhang stilvoller Handarbeiten.* Stuttgart: Deutsche Verlags-Anstalt, 1893.

Stuhlmann, A. *Stickmuster für Schule und Haus.* 2 vols. Stuttgart and Berlin: W. Spemann, 1890†.

Teschendorff, Toni. *Kreuzstich-muster für Leinenstickerei.* Berlin: Ernest Wasmuth, 1879.

Vorlagen für Handarbeiten von Häkelspitzen und Mignardisen. N.p., ca. 1880.

Wiener Mode. *Album der Monogramme für kreuzstich.* Vienna and Leipzig: Verlag der "Wiener Mode," 1894.

———. *Häkelmuster-album der "Wiener Mode."* Vienna: Verlag der "Wiener Mode," [1896].

———. *Sammlung gehäkelter Spitzen und Einsätze.* Vienna: Verlag de "Wiener Mode," [1896].

Part 5: Periodicals

United States

Art Amateur. Edited by Montague Marks. New York: Montague Marks, 1879–1900†.

Art Interchange. Edited by William Whitlock. New York: Society of Decorative Art, 1878–1900†.

Arthur's Home Magazine. Philadelphia: T. S. Arthur & Co., 1852–1898.

The Delineator. New York: Butterick Co., 1873–1900†.

Dorcas. New York: Howard Brothers & Co., 1884–1886.

Florence Home Needlework. Florence, Mass.: Florence Publishing Co., 1887–1896.

Frank Leslie's Ladies' Gazette of Fashion and Fancy Needlework. [Philadelphia?]: Frank Leslie, 1854–1857.

Godey's Lady's Book (title varies). New York: Godey Co., 1830–1898.

Harper's Bazar. New York: Harper, 1867–1900†.

Home Art. Edited by Adelaide E. Heron. Chicago: Home Art Publishing Co., 1885–1900†.

Home Needlework Magazine. Florence, Mass: Florence Publishing Co., 1899–1900†.

The Home-maker. New York: Home-maker Co., 1888–1893.

Ingalls' Home Magazine. Edited by Lida and M. J. Clarkson. Lynn, Mass.: J. F. Ingalls, 1887–1891.

Ladies American Magazine. New York: Henry White, 1859.

Ladies' Fancywork Magazine. Grand Rapids, Mich., 1900†.

Ladies Home Journal and Practical Housekeeper. New York: Curtis Publishing Co., 1883–1900†.

The Modern Priscilla. Lynn, Mass., 1887–1900†.

Peterson's Magazine. Philadelphia: C. J. Peterson, 1842–1898.

Great Britain

The Englishwoman's Domestic Magazine. 1852–1879.

Lady's Album of Fancy Work. London, ca. 1850.

Myra's Journal of Dress and Needlework. 1875†.

The Needle. Edited by E. Riego de la Branchardière. London, 1853.

France

Bijou. Paris: E. Ludewig, 1851.

La Brodeuse. Paris, 1834–1841.

Cendrillon. Paris, 1850–1872.

Le Guide-Sajou. Paris, 1851–1854.

Germany

Der Bazar. 1869–1899.

Journal für moderne Stickerei, Mode und Weibliche Handarbeiten. Weimar: N. von Herder, 1851–1855.

Selected Bibliography

General Works

Bath, Virginia Churchill. *Needlework in America: History, Designs, and Techniques.* New York: Viking Press, 1979.

De Pauw, Linda Grant, and Conover Hunt. *Remember the Ladies: Women in America, 1750–1815.* New York: Viking Press, 1976.

Hanley, Hope. *Needlepoint in America.* New York: Charles Scribner's Sons, 1969.

Harbeson, Georgiana Brown. *American Needlework: The History of Decorative Stitchery and Embroidery from the Late Sixteenth to Twentieth Century.* New York: Coward-McCann, 1938; reprint ed., New York: Bonanza Books, 1961.

Lichten, Frances. *Decorative Art of the Victorian Era.* New York: Charles Scribner's Sons, 1950.

Morris, Barbara. *Victorian Embroidery* ["Victorian Collector Series"]. New York: Thomas Nelson & Sons, 1962.

Schiffer, Margaret B. *Historic Needlework of Pennsylvania.* New York: Charles Scribner's Sons, 1968.

Swan, Susan Burrows. *A Winterthur Guide to American Needlework.* New York: Crown Publishers, 1976.

————. *Plain and Fancy.* New York: Holt, Rinehart and Winston, 1977.

Synge, Lanto. *Antique Needlework.* Poole, England: Blandford Press, 1982.

Warren, Geoffrey. *A Stitch in Time: Victorian and Edwardian Needlecraft.* New York: Taplinger Publishing Company, 1976.

Weisman, Judith Reiter, and Wendy Lavitt. *Labors of Love: America's Textiles and Needlework, 1650–1930.* New York: Alfred A. Knopf, 1987.

Wheeler, Candace T. *The Development of Embroidery in America.* New York and London: Harper & Brothers, 1921.

Wiczyk, Arlene Zeger, comp. *A Treasury of Needlework Projects from Godey's Lady's Book.* New York: Arco, 1972.

Samplers

Bolton, Ethel Stanwood and Eva Johnston Coe. *American Samplers.* Boston: Massachusetts Society of the Colonial Dames of America, 1921.

Krueger, Glee F. *A Gallery of Samplers: The Theodore H. Kapnek Collection.* New York: E. P. Dutton, 1978.

———. *New England Samplers to 1840.* Sturbridge, Mass.: Old Sturbridge Village, 1978.

Ring, Betty. *Let Virtue Be a Guide to Thee: Needlework in the Education of Rhode Island Women, 1730–1830.* Providence: Rhode Island Historical Society, 1983.

———. *American Needlework Treasures; Samplers and Silk Embroideries from the Collection of Betty Ring.* New York: E. P. Dutton and Museum of American Folk Art, 1987.

Muslin Work

Davis, Mildred J. *Embroidery Designs, 1780–1820: From the Manuscript Collection of the Textile Resource and Research Center of the Valentine Museum* [Richmond, Va.] New York: Crown Publishers, 1971.

Canvas Work

Müller, Heidi. *Rosen, Tulpen, Nelken . . . : Stickvorlagen des 19. Jahrhunderts aus Deutschland und Österreich.* Berlin: Museum für Deutsche Volkskunde, 1977.

Proctor, Molly G. *Victorian Canvas Work: Berlin Wool Work.* London: B. T. Batsford, 1972.

Crazy Patchwork

McMorris, Penny. *Crazy Quilts.* New York: E. P. Dutton, 1984.

Pennsylvania German Hand Towels

Gehret, Ellen J. *This Is the Way I Pass My Time.* Birdsboro, Pa.: Pennsylvania German Society, 1985.

Quilts

Bishop, Robert, and Patricia Coblentz. *New Discoveries in American Quilts.* New York: E. P. Dutton, 1975.

Ferrero, Pat; Elaine Hedges; and Julie Silber. *Hearts and Hands: The Influence of Women and Quilts on American Society.* San Francisco: Quilt Digest Press, 1987.

Holstein, Jonathan. *The Pieced Quilt: An American Design Tradition.* Boston: New York Graphic Society, 1973.

Lasansky, Jeannette. *In the Heart of Pennsylvania: Nineteenth & Twentieth Century Quiltmaking Traditions.* Lewisburg, Pa.: Oral Traditions Project of the Union County Historical Society, 1985.

Lipsett, Linda Otto. *Remember Me: Women and Their Friendship Quilts.* San Francisco: Quilt Digest Press, 1985.

Orlofsky, Patsy, and Myron Orlofsky. *Quilts in America.* New York: McGraw-Hill, 1974.

Safford, Carleton L., and Robert Bishop. *America's Quilts and Coverlets.* New York: E. P. Dutton, 1972.

Hooked and Sewn Rugs

Kopp, Joel, and Kate Kopp. *American Hooked and Sewn Rugs: Folk Art Underfoot.* New York: E. P. Dutton, 1975.

Museum of American Folk Art. *Hooked Rugs in the Folk Art Tradition.* New York: Museum of American Folk Art, 1974.

von Rosenstiel, Helene. *American Rugs and Carpets: From the Seventeenth Century to Modern Times.* New York: William Morrow, 1978.

Index